My
From]

This book is dedicated to the two women who have ... o thrive as a United States Marine. First, my wonderful Mother Mary Bushey, who never ceased to believe in and support me in my desire to be a Marine, and who was a wonderful support system during her entire life. Secondly, but no less significant, my wonderful wife Cathy Bushey who, despite absences and hardships, always supported her USMC husband in every way.

And

The **"Make A Wish Foundation,"** a phenomenal organization that works so hard and effectively to bring happiness to very special children, and who will receive 100% of the revenue from this book.

Introduction

This book is about a little boy who never lost focus on what he hoped to achieve in life: to become a United States Marine. From my very first coherent thoughts as a toddler, I just knew that I would be a Marine. As I grew up, it was an absolute accepted fact that I would not complete conventional high school, because I would be entering boot camp on my 17th birthday, which would occur during my junior year. With a minor exception, that is exactly what occurred; the exception was that my birthday fell on a Sunday, and I could not leave for the Marine Corps Recruit Depot until reaching the old age of seventeen years and one day!

As a boy growing up, I was typically described as a decent kid, but someone who did not put adequate effort into my studies. I left high school with a dismal academic record of mostly weak and failing grades; three months later I graduated from basic training as the platoon's honor man! Several months later I graduated from Communications School with the highest grades of anyone from my battalion. Subsequent to enlisted service, I entered college, kept a full time job on the side, and was on the academic honor role for most of my studies up to and including my master's degree. Something sure as hell happened, and that something was the United States Marine Corps.

This book is not about my combat experiences. I wish it were so, but the reality is that I encountered very little military conflict during all of my years of Marine Corps service. When my grandkids want me to reminisce about my combat service, I respond that I don't want to talk about it, and then reluctantly and sadly add that there really isn't much to talk about. I did serve on the ground at Guantanamo Bay during the 1962 Missile Crisis. While in the Western Pacific during the early stages of the Vietnam War, my service amounted to little more than a few courier trips into and out of Danang. By the time I reentered the Corps as an officer, Vietnam was winding down and my services in that theatre were not needed. During the 1991 War in the Persian Gulf I commanded 3D ANGLICO and, with the main body, was activated just as the 56-hour war came to an end; fortunately, my advanced party did get into the fray and destroyed 230 Iraqi armored vehicles. In 2004 my application to return to active duty, from retired status, was approved and I had orders to the staff of the 2nd Marine Division in Iraq; but the orders were cancelled several days before I was to report to the Mobilization Training Battalion, as the Marine Corps changed the policy and cancelled recall waivers for any retiree who had reached the age of sixty. Among my few true disappointments in life is my failure to serve my country and Corps in conventional combat. Damn, I sure tried! I guess the blood and guts and death and destruction of over four decades as a cop will have to fill that void.

What this book does offer the reader are scores and scores of true and unique experiences in my approximately 38 years of being a Marine, regular and reserve, officer and enlisted. This is the story of a high school dropout who ultimately became a full colonel, and all of the unique situations that contributed to that ascent. From the trials and tribulations of boot camp to barracks life in the states and the Orient, from harsh field exercises in the California desert to the steamy jungles of the Caribbean and Asia, to the making of both an NCO and later an officer, and everything in between, this is a book that has some pretty interesting stories. A word of warning, there are some situations that are neither pleasant nor politically correct, but there is nothing that is not 100% true.

Very honestly, I had doubts that I would ever make corporal, let alone eventually become a commissioned officer. I was not born with a silver spoon in my mouth, and did not always perform as well as was expected. I made mistakes, a lot of them, but never stopped "leaning forward," and never lost either my spirit or my commitment. When I slipped and fell, which was often, I picked myself up, dusted myself off, and continued to march. While there was some proficiency and merit involved, I must be candid in acknowledging that luck and timing were also essential ingredients in the successes that I achieved.

If you want to be a Marine, wish you had been a Marine, or know a Marine, this book is for you. Enjoy!

Note: This book is a greatly expanded and modified version of the USMC portion of *The Many Forks In My Many Roads*, written by the same author and published in 2012.

Contents

	Introduction	2
1.	Being a Marine Was In the Genes	6
2.	Adolescent Years – USMC Style	11
3.	Early Teen Years – USMC Style	19
4.	Entering the Marine Corps	21
5.	Boot Camp	23
6.	2nd Infantry Training Regiment	36
7.	Second Battalion, First Marine Regiment (2/1)	38
8.	The Cuban Missile Crisis	51
9.	Back to Camp Pendleton	61
10.	The Orient – 3rd Battalion, 9th Marine Regiment (3/9)	68
11.	Marine Corps Air Station – El Toro	90
12.	Post Enlisted Service and Civilian Jobs	100
13.	Becoming a Commissioned Officer	141
14.	Fourth Light Anti-Air Missile Battalion	145
15.	14th Counterintelligence Team	147
16.	3D Air-Naval Gunfire Liaison Company	154
17.	Fourth Forward Area Air Defense Battalion	169
18.	Marine Air Support Squadron Four	181
19.	Mobilization Training Unit CA-49	188
20.	3D Air-Naval Gunfire Liaison Company	190

21.	4th Marine Division Staff	210
22.	I Marine Expeditionary Force	227
23.	Post USMC Retirement Thoughts & Actions	229
Epilogue		232

Chapter One
BEING A MARINE WAS IN THE GENES!

In this part, I will discuss military-related thoughts and actions that took place from the time I can first recall anything until roughly age ten.

My Earliest Recollection

I honestly cannot recall any time in my life, since I have had coherent thoughts, when I wasn't obsessed with the desire to be a United States Marine. From the time I was just a small child until the day that I took the enlistment oath, it was clearly known and accepted by my entire family that I was going to enter the Marine Corps on my 17th birthday. I don't even recall a conversation about finishing high school, as it was just an accepted reality that I would finish high school in the military. As it turned out, that is almost exactly what occurred; the only glitch was that my 17th birthday was on a Sunday, and I was unable to be sworn until the next day!

My Brother – A United States Marine

There is no doubt that my brother initiated what became an obsession on my part to become a Marine. Laurence David Bushey (RIP). Born in 1932, he was twelve years older than me and, like my subsequent actions, he quit high school when he was seventeen and in 1950 enlisted in the Marine Corps. His initial USMC service coincided with my first coherent thoughts. He was initially stationed at the Marine Barracks in San Francisco and was able to come home on some weekends, and always brought me some USMC goody such as a belt, hat, or emblem. I cherished these items and was very proud of my Marine brother.

When I became a Marine, I used some of the items that my brother had given me when I was a child. His eagle, globe and anchor insignias were on my covers, (hats), his metal PFC stripes were on my utilities, (uniforms), and one of his belt buckles was the one that I wore during my entire USMC service. I still cherish these items.

A Nun Took My Eagle, Globe and Anchor

One of my early tragedies involved my next-door neighbor, another kid whose name was George Derby. One day he borrowed my USMC hat emblem so that he could take it to his school and show it to the other students during the classroom "Share Session." He attended a Catholic school and his teacher, a nun, apparent felt that the military insignia was an inappropriate item to bring to school, and confiscated it from him. On another occasion, he also borrowed an old authentic police badge that I had obtained at a second hand store, and that too was confiscated by the same nun. I never got either item back, and was very troubled by my loss of both of these items. In fact, I am still pissed about the actions of that nun!

Military Patches in Cereal Boxes

World War II was still a pretty recent event when I was a small child, and military surplus was in great abundance. One of the major makers of breakfast cereals took advantage of this reality by placing mint army unit shoulder patches in each box of cereal, as a marking strategy. I thought this was great, and ate a great deal of cereal, often two bowls a day, so I could get my hands on the patch in the next box!

Collecting Military Patches & Insignia

I have collected various things throughout my life, but my very first hobby was collecting military insignias of every type, both cloth and metal. As previously mentioned, both World War II and Korea were recent events (the Korean War was still raging when I start collecting military items) and military items were in abundance and could be found everywhere. Every household included a veteran and every garage contained sea bags and locker boxes full of uniforms and other military goodies. Just about every community had a military surplus store that was chock full of real military items. I have always had a bit of an obsessive side on issues of interest, and this trait resulted in me having a great collection of military insignia. Before about age ten, I could identify any insignia or medal of any American branch of service of service!

Collecting Military Uniforms

Collecting medals and insignias wasn't enough for me; I had to collect the uniforms as well! Like other military surplus, uniforms of all branches were in great abundance and could be obtained for next to nothing. While always too large for me to wear (then!), if a shirt or jacket had a neat insignia, I found a way to obtain it. I also got a great many uniform items from my various uncles who served in World War II.

Watching My Brother Leave for Korea

In 1953, while the Korean War was still being fought, my parents and I went to San Diego and watched my brother leave for Korea on the U.S.S. Mann, a troopship. The ship set sail from a military berth at the base of Broadway Street. As the ship left the dock, we were able to spot Larry among the hundreds of other Marines, and to wave goodbye. It was an emotional time for me, and I cried at the departure of my brother. Ten years later, as a young Marine enroute to the Far East, I set sail from the same dock aboard a similar troopship, the U.S.S. Patrick, but said my goodbyes to my family at our home in Duarte, and specifically asked them not to come and watch the ship depart; I wanted to avoid the tears and the drama.

A Saint Christopher's Medal from Oceanside

On the way home from San Diego after watching my brother's ship depart for Korea, we stopped in downtown Oceanside where my parents let me browse in one of the military supply stores. They bought me a sterling Saint Christopher's Medal that I have to this day, and which I wore attached to my dog tags during my entire 38 years of Marine Corps service. In 1991, subsequent to the First Gulf War, when on active duty and stationed at Camp Pendleton, I reunited with the wonderful folks who sold my parents the medal in 1953! The H&M Military Store was still owned by Harry and Mary Cathey. While on active duty at that time, Harry and Mary became dear friends and it was during a conversation that I told them of the medal purchase in 1953, at which time Harry asked to see the medal (it was on my dog tags hanging around my neck), and immediately identified it as one that their store had carried years before! While I cannot honestly recall the details of the purchase, the store was on a corner, and that was the store. What a coincidence! Harry passed away several years ago, but Mary and I remain friends to this day, and I never go to or though Oceanside without visiting with her.

Kicked Out of the Cub Scouts

The Cub Scout career was short and undistinguished. I had only been in the Pack for a short time when I got into some type of fight with the den mother's son. As a result, the den mother called my mother just before a meeting and told her that I was a disruptive influence and that perhaps a sabbatical from the scouts would be a good idea. She also reminded my mother that it was my turn to bring the donuts to the meeting, and if I was not going to be attending the meeting, my mom was still obligated to provide the donuts! My mom drove me to a donut shop, got a box of donuts, then went to the den mother's house where my mom told me to give the woman the donuts and tell them that I was too good for the rest of them. Upon arrival home, I took all the Cub Scout patches off my uniform and replaced them with Marine Corps patches, and wore the shirt proudly for all to see. I can still recall wearing my USMC adorned former cub scout shirt while sitting on a fire hydrant near my house and not being disturbed in the least at a couple of other kids who were making fun of my new attire. I occasionally drive past my old home in Alhambra and never cease to glance at that same fire hydrant with a smile on my face.

Learning to Shoot

Guns have always been part of my life. As a small child, Christmas and birthdays always yielded rifles and pistols. My brother gave me my first air rifle (pellet gun) when I was about eight years old. Shortly after that, I got my first BB gun. As a youth, I fired thousands and thousands of bb's and pellets, and became a very deadly shot (as the souls of hundred of birds can attest). Note: I am truly remorseful for the hundred of birds and rabbits that I have shot in my lifetime and, while a strong supporter of legal hunting, I no longer have the appetite to shoot any living thing (except in combat or criminals in the commission of a crime).

Leggings & Blue Jeans

The abundance of surplus available when I was a kid included leggings of every shape, style, and color. I frequently wore them over my blue jeans and tennis shoes. Seldom would I go the movies and see a war movie without being attired in my favorite leggings.

Little Doughboys in the Alfalfa Field

My collection of uniforms included several heavy wool tunics from World War I, along with the doughboy helmets and equipment used during that era. I still recall "playing war" at night in the alfalfa field that used to exist in Baldwin Park on the site where the California Highway Patrol now has a station. There were some pretty hot summer nights where it would seem that those heavy wool coats with high collars would have been pretty uncomfortable, but my recollections are nothing but a lot of fun! My "equipment" consisted of my "03" Springfield training rifle, a gas mask in a canvas bag strapped to my waist, and a complete cartridge belt with a canteen, first aid packet, and holster for my replica .45 semi-automatic pistol. Sergeant York would have been proud of me!

Chapter 2
ADOLESCENT YEARS – USMC STYLE

In this chapter I will discuss military thoughts and actions that took place from roughly age ten to thirteen.

Storming the Beach at Playa Del Rey

Dorothy and Matthew Twomey, my mom's sister and brother-in-law, were two of the finest individuals a person could hope for as an aunt and uncle. In the last 1950s, Matt and Dot lived on a hillside between Los Angeles International Airport (LAX) and the beach at Playa Del Rey, and I was fortunate to be able to spend considerable time with them during the summer and on school vacations. At the time, the beach was pretty rough with dirt berms, and not a place that drew many visitors. For me, however, it was heaven. I always took a sea bag full of uniforms, combat equipment, my helmet, and my Lee Enfield Training Rifle (the actual weight of the real Lee Enfield Rifle, which is very realistic, and something that I still possess). I spent hours storming the beach, running, crawling, and engaging a mythical enemy. I was motivated in part because of watching similar scenes in various movies (especially "Sands of Iwo Jima" and the television series, "Victory at Sea").

These homes have long been torn down because of LAX noise abatement, but on the many occasions where I fly into and out of LAX, I am able to look down at the remaining remnants of the streets and see almost exactly where Matt and Dot's home used to be. Matt served in the Navy CBs (Construction Battalions) during World War II, and experienced horrible bouts with the residuals of Malaria for his entire life, having spent approximately three years in combat in the South Pacific, much of it under terrible tropical conditions with hoards of mosquitoes, 100 degree humidity, decaying human bodies, etc. I have every confidence that heaven is a better place because Matt and Dot are there.

In the Field – City of Hope and the Santa Fe Dam

While I lived in a number of locations while growing up, I consider the small town of Duarte to have been my home town, and where we lived was a virtual dream come true for a kid who had a fascination with the outdoors and who wanted to "play Marine." We lived at the bottom of a dead end street (Cinco Robles), alongside the City of Hope National Medical Center, and at the edge of the massive Santa Fe Dam. The dam occupied hundreds of acres and was truly a wild and desolate place, and was perfect for carrying out my obsessive military fantasies, hiking, and shooting my trusty BB gun. Without exaggeration, and like clockwork, all day during the summer and after school during the rest of the year, me and my dog Gretel, went into the dam. While it is now a recreation area open to the public, it was then sacred U. S. property, closed to the public, and with trespassing taken seriously by the asshole guard who had a home on the premises. He would sometimes spot and try to catch me before I could get outside the boundary fence, and on the single occasion when he caught me threatened to shoot my dog and confiscate my BB gun. I loved that place.

As mentioned, the property now belongs to the County of Los Angeles and constitutes the Santa Fe Dam Recreation Area. Our little daughter has spent quite a bit of time there in her Junior Lifeguard Program, and I spend some time immediately adjacent to it when I give my O Negative pint of blood ever 56 days at the City of Hope National Medical Center. Moreover, I drive over that sacred ground (sacred to me) on a daily basis as the 605 Freeway now passes right through my old play area. I can also still make out the remnants of the house where the asshole guard lived.

Buying an Antique Treadle Sewing Machine

As a kid, from my early elementary years, I would acquire military patches, old military uniforms, and hand-sew the patches on my clothing. About the time I was in the 6th grade, in Duarte, my sewing activities really went into high gear. While browsing at a second hand store in Monrovia, I found an old Singer Treadle sewing machine, and bought it for $5.00. Within a week or so, I had mastered the use of that wonderful machine and became somewhat of a master at removing and replacing patches, shortening sleeves, and repairing canvas equipment. I spent hundreds of hours on that machine, and considered it to be one of the true wonders of the world.

This machine turned out to be a good financial investment as well. Up until the time I went into the military, I would often make custom items for folks, including wheel covers for auto body shops (to prevent paint from reaching the tires when a car was being painted and repaired), and custom carpenter aprons for workmen at construction sites. For my first couple of years in the Marine Corps, I also made a few bucks on the side, while in the States, such as replacing old stripes with new insignias when fellow Marines were promoted.

The San Gabriel Valley Junior Marines

In about 1956, while living on Donaldale Street in Puente (now La Puente), I joined an outfit known as the San Gabriel Valley Young Marines Drill Team. A former Marine formed the outfit, and we wore old Air Force uniforms (I guess old Marine uniforms were not available) with specially made Junior Marine patches. I just loved the affiliation, and in the many parades that we marched in, the Marine Corps-oriented meetings, and the field trips. After a couple of years there was a parental battle where control was wrestled from the founder, Jim Smith, and the organization taken over by Mr. and Mrs. Little, whose son George was among the other kids in the outfit. My parents did not care for the adult Little's and I did not care for little George, and that was the end of my affiliation with the Junior Marines.

Years later, as a colonel on a two week active duty assignment to a massive field exercise at the Marine Base in Twenty-Nine Palms, Sergeant Major George Little, USMCR, was assigned as my sergeant major! We had quite a reunion, with a lot of stories being exchanged, and absolutely none of the hostility that had existed years before. At the time, George was a sergeant with the Alameda (CA.) County Sheriff's Department. Not long after our two weeks together, he died as a result of an accidental fall unrelated to his sheriff's position. RIP Sergeant Major Little.

Devastated at Inability to Attend Devil Pups

In 1954, Duncan Shaw, Sr. established Devil Pups, Inc.; he was a World War 1 Marine veteran who went on to became a successful businessman and civic leader in Los Angeles. Duncan and other leaders who played a role in the program's development, including former Los Angeles Police Chief William H. Parker, had a vision that the fiber of society could be strengthened by creating the opportunity for young men to attend a ten-day Summer encampment at the Marine Corps Base, Camp Pendleton, where USMC values could be instilled and citizenship principles reinforced. A couple of years later, in 1956, I was in the San Gabriel Valley Junior Marines and our adult leader, former Marine Jim Smith, was affiliated with Devil Pups and had the ability to send youngsters. Smith was big in the American Legion and decided that he would use Devil Pups as a recruiting tool; if the father would join his post he would send the kid to Devil Pups. Both my dad and my brother were veterans, but my dad was sick and hospitalized and my brother did not want to join the American Legion; as a result, all of my close pals went to Devil Pups, but I was not permitted to attend. I cried myself to sleep on the night that I was told that I could not attend. Note: I am now one of the vice presidents of Devil Pups, have been with the organization since 1970, and am a generous benefactor of that wonderful organization.

Weekend at Marine Corps Air Station, El Toro

During my tenure in the Young Marines, we had a weekend field trip to the Marine Corps Air Station at El Toro, California. Those two days were about as close to heaven as I had been in my young life to that point! We really didn't do anything that significant: looked and went aboard a few transport planes and ate in a mess hall, but it was a bona-fide Marine Corps experience nonetheless. We were billeted in an old bachelor officer quarters building, (B.O.Q.), but to me it might just as well have been the Waldorf Astoria. Years later, as a Marine lieutenant, I stayed in the same building, and never entered that structure without walking past the room where I had stayed during my Young Marines field trip.

Creating Belleau Woods from Christmas Trees

Creating a suitable battlefield in the backyard of the suburban Alhambra home where I lived was pretty tough, but I came up with a unique solution right after Christmas in the early 1950s. I was fascinated with the stories of Marine heroism during the World War I Belleau Woods Campaign, and saw all Christmas trees being discarded as the solution to creating my own forest battleground. It was just a day or two after Christmas and my parents had gone to work (I was one of those latchkey kids) when I used my red wagon to collect scores of discarded Christmas trees, and created a literal forest in the backyard of our home. There could not have been less than at least fifty trees, and probably many more than that, spread across our fairly small rear yard. It was great and gave me several hours of fun – until my parents came home. I don't recall them being terribly upset, but within minutes I was returning the Christmas trees to the trash piles in front of the other homes in the neighborhood. I suspect that my mom and dad got a laugh out of this situation.

Memorizing the Rank Structures and Awards

The key to understanding the military was to understand the rank structure, insignias, and awards of *all* branches of the military. Without exaggeration, I had memorized and could recite all of this information by the time I was about ten years old! Most of the initial information came from a National Geographic magazine published during World War II, and within several months it was ragged and dog-eared, but something that I treated like a bible.

Memorizing the Semaphore Alphabet & Signals

Without abandoning my commitment to become a Marine, I also had somewhat of a fascination with the Navy. During one of my periods of studying the Navy, I taught myself the entire semaphore alphabet, and spent time practicing sending signals with a set of surplus signal flags.

Memorizing the Rules of the Road at Sea

Our first home in Duarte was a stucco rental on an acre that the owner, George Barnes, called the "Lazy Y" Ranch. George was originally from England, and had served in the Royal Navy during World War I. He was a wonderful man and colorful character that often told me stories about his military service. One day he offered to teach me the Royal Navy's "Rules of the Road at Sea," which reflected the international rules governing maritime operations. Within a week or so, I memorized verbatim this complex paragraph, and to this day am able to recite it flawlessly.

When upon a port is seen, a steamer's starboard light of green. There is not so much for you to do, for green to port keeps clear of you. Green-to-green or Red-to-red, perfect safety, go ahead. But if to your port red appears, it is your duty to keep clear. Act is judgment, says is proper, ease her back and stop her. If in danger with no room to turn, ease her, stop her, go astern.

Throughout my life there have been a number of persons who have been left nearly speechless, as I have recited this historic, but still valid information.

Fascination With West Point and Annapolis

Some of my favorite movies portrayed cadet and midshipmen activities at the Military and Naval Academies. As a lousy student in humble surroundings, the thought of ever being able to attend a service academy was something that never crossed my mind, as I just knew that I would never be qualified. Nonetheless, my interest was strong and I read and watched everything I could find. At one point, I spent about a week carefully sewing a dark blue band around the bill of a navy uniform hat, to replicate the hats worn by midshipmen at the Naval Academy at Annapolis, Maryland. During that same era, I also meticulously cut out and applied the very large sergeant's stripes for a West Point uniform; a sewing job that Betsy Ross would have been envious of!

Interestingly, when later commissioned, I served with a number of fine men who were Naval Academy graduates, and actually by-passed several of them in performance and advancement. In no instance did any of them advance beyond me. To this day, I have the highest regard for our service academies, but now realize that the graduates are not super human, but mortal souls just like the rest of us. However, those men and women who have graduated from any of the service academies have much to be justifiably proud of, and I wish that I had been one of them!

Visiting Used Book Stores

To say that I enjoyed visiting used bookstores would be an understatement. Almost without exception, these bookstores were full of military books and manuals, and I spend hours poring over old musty books in pursuit of information pertaining to my areas of interest, primarily Marine Corps and Navy history and procedures.

Most of the used bookstores that I visited were in downtown Los Angeles, where I frequently ventured by myself on public transportation buses.

Obsession With Surplus Stores

There was nowhere on earth that I would rather have been than inside a surplus store. Subsequent to World War II, surplus military items became big business, and just about every community had a surplus store. They were all over the place, and I knew every one of them within several miles of where I lived. Beyond what was on the shelves, the owners were constantly acquiring new items based on frequent governmental surplus sales. My whole life consisted of helmets, gas masks, cartridge belts, canteens, backpacks, field radios, switchboards, and related items. My grade school allowance from my parents was fifty cents each week, and was typically spent at a surplus store.

My Favorite Odor

The smell of surplus military canvas! Pure and simple. Those who see this as a sign of adolescence sickness may be right!

Our Family Vacations – San Diego

I was fortunate to have loving parents who tolerated my fascination with the military. While my family had been very prosperous in the 1940s, we had fallen on hard times when I was a toddler. We took two or three short family vacations, which consisted of two nights at a motel in San Diego, a trip to Tijuana (Mexico), and a couple of days where I walked up and down Broadway Street watching the Marines and Sailors and scrounging discarded military patches from the floors of the many tailor shops that catered to service personnel. Our family could not afford anything more than these brief San Diego visits, but to me there was nowhere that I would rather have gone.

The One (Only!) Successful School Year

To say that I was a poor student is an understatement. From first grade through what little high school I intended, with one exception, I was a lousy student. Moreover, my attendance was chronically poor as well. The one exception was the 6th grade where I attended Van Wig Elementary School in Puente (now La Puente), California. Our teacher, Mr. Wilson, was a man (all my other teachers up to that point had been women), and he was an Army veteran who had served in the Korean War and obtained his degree through the G.I. Bill. On the first hour of the first day in class, as he was explaining his expectations, I made some stupid remark that really triggered his anger. He grabbed me by my shirt, yanked me out of my chair, dragged me out of the room, jacked me up against a brick wall, called me a "little shithead," and made it clear that he was not going to tolerate my foolish behavior! My behavior, grades, and attendance were good all year, and I worshipped the ground that Mr. Wilson walked on. Several years ago I tried unsuccessfully to locate Mr. Wilson and tell him about the very positive effect he had on me, but there were too many Robert Wilsons and, even with the efforts of the superintendent of the Bassett School District, I had no luck. I occasionally drive by Bassett School and always look at the brick wall where Mr. Wilson jacked up that little shithead.

Chapter 3
EARLY TEEN YEARS – USMC STYLE

In this chapter I will discuss military-related thoughts and actions that took place from roughly age thirteen to roughly age sixteen.

Hitchhiking in a Sailor Uniform

Don Middleton was one of my best high school pals, and he was just as obsessed with joining the Navy as I was with joining the Marine Corps. For whatever reason, my supply of military stuff included several completed navy uniforms. One Saturday night, Don and I put on navy uniforms and started hitchhiking around the San Gabriel Valley. The uniforms were perfect in every respect, worn well, shined shoes, and identified both of us having the rank of seaman apprentice. One of the cars that stopped and give us a ride was being driven by a real live Navy chief petty officer, in full uniform! Fortunately, Don and I knew enough about the military as to sound credible in the brief conversation that took place during the ride. We were very relieved when that ride was over! For years after that, including when a real Lance Corporal Bushey visited a real Petty Officer 2nd Class in Yokosuka (Japan), we laughed about the incident.

This situation gives rise to the question of why I did not go hitchhiking in a Marine uniform; simple; it would be pretty hard to truly impersonate a Marine! Marines have that special look that is a combination of a truly unique haircut, sunburned or well-tanned heads beneath where a cover (hat) is placed, razor-sharp uniform seams, spit- shined shoes, and a truly confident demeanor. Without criticizing the demeanor and sharp appearance of most sailors, the appearance of the typical Marine borders on the obsessive and is not easily replicated by a stupid kid.

Alterations to a Navy Uniform – Oops!

While still in high school, I became great friends with a real live sailor. Dale Butler was assigned to a Heavy cruiser that was home ported in San Diego, and would visit my home on many weekends. He was impressed with my sewing skills, and I also mistakenly thought that my skills as a tailor were pretty good. At his request, I gladly took in the seams of his uniform jumpers, so that they would fit nice and snug. All was well until the first time he laundered the jumpers. I didn't know much about creating a legitimate seam, and had just taken the excess material in, ran a stitch up and down to keep it together, and cut off the excess material. The sides of all of his jumpers unraveled while still in the wash, and were ruined. Dale and I remained great friends over the years, but he did not ask me to alter anymore of his uniforms.

Dropping out of High School

As mentioned previously, it was an absolute accepted fact that I was going to enter the Marine Corps on my 17th birthday, and would seek to complete high school while in the military. Although I started my junior year at Duarte High School, I really don't know why, because I only had a couple of month before turning seventeen, and would be gone. I only lasted a couple of weeks before quitting and going full-time at the Monarch Body Shop in Monrovia, where I had been a part-time "whatever," (prepping cars for painting, driving a tow truck, and *whatever* minor task came along). I worked this job right up until the day I left for boot camp.

Preparing For Boot Camp

Realistically, because of my obsessive interest in the military, I had been preparing for the Marine Corps since I was a small child. My brother went into the Marine Corps in 1950, when I was about six years old, and I have been enthusiastic about the military since then. My greatest joys were going to surplus stores, of which there were many because a great deal of military surplus was available after World War II. For about three months before my 17th birthday, I studied everything that I could find about the Marine Corps. I had the *Guidebook For Marines* and knew it cold. I knew the General Orders, Field Sanitation & Hygiene, History & Traditions, all the field pack configurations, First Aid, Rank Structure, etc., etc. My brother borrowed an M-1 Garand Rife from someone, and taught me to identify every part and to field strip it blindfolded! When I went into the Marine Corps, on my 17th birthday like I always knew that I would, I really knew my stuff.

Chapter Four
ENTERING THE MARINE CORPS

Driven Downtown By My Dad

During the wee small hours of Monday morning, November 13th, 1961, my Dad drive me Downtown to the Military Induction & Processing Center at 1031 South Broadway Street. He pulled up right in front, kissed me goodbye, wished me well, and drove off. I will never forget that moment, and also never drive past that location without looking at the exact spot where my father dropped me off.

Interestingly, that building was then, and later owned by Jack Needleman, a businessman I got to know and developed a friendship with many years later, when I was the commanding officer of Central Area.

Obtaining a Waiver in Order to Enlist

My arrest for burglary and period of juvenile probation became somewhat of an issue, and for a while it appeared that it may have prevented, or at least delayed my enlistment into the Marine Corps. I needed a waiver. I was ushered into the office of a Marine major, and interviewed about the incident, what I had done since the incident to become a better citizen, and why I wanted to enter the Marine Corps. Apparently I said the right things, because a waiver was granted then and there.

My sin was not exactly the crime of the century, but it was a burglary. Myself and a couple of my pals found a broken door to the gym at Duarte High School, and were able to squeeze through the opening, which was secured with a chain, and get inside the building. Once in, we each took a football jersey. Unfortunately, the sister of one of my pals, who disliked all of us, called the Sheriff's Department. After sitting in a cell at the Temple City Sheriff's Station for a few hours, my parents came and secured my freedom. While I never went to court, I was placed on probation for several months.

"Don't Bother To Re-Type The Form"

When completing the enlistment paperwork, I enlisted for four years, but before being sworn in, learned that I could go for three years if my written score was high enough, so I approached the clerical sergeant and asked if I could change my contract to three years. He was indignant and said I scored high enough, but that he would have to type a form over, so I apologized and told him four was fine (boy, did I kick myself three years later when all my friends were getting out – but four years worked out for the best anyway). Regardless, the sergeant got nice again.

Sworn In & Sweep The Decks

In mid-afternoon, the group of us was sworn into the United States Marine Corps. My "pal," the sergeant who had previously been nice when I told him not to retype the form, immediately started screaming at me, threw me a broom, and told me to "sweep the deck!" So much for my new friend the sergeant, and welcome to the Marine Corps! It was at this time that I was assigned my enlisted serial number: 1989579.

Four years was fine

Chapter Five
BOOT CAMP

A Unique Welcome at the Bus Station

I and about a dozen other young men were put on a Greyhound by the folks at the Armed Forces Processing Station in Los Angeles with San Diego as our destination. Upon arrival in San Diego, we were met by a couple of stern and mean Marine staff sergeants (should I have expected anything else?) They herded us into the back of a camper shell on a USMC truck and, once inside, started whacking at us with a swagger stick! There were no injuries, but I think we all wondered why these guys had to hit us. We were driven straight to the Recruit Receiving Barracks. Like generations of new jarheads before us, we line-up and stood on the "yellow footprints," and went through the initial process of clothing and necessities issuance, showers, temporary berthing assignments, and then assembled into recruit platoons and introductions (if you can call screaming at us an introduction) to our drill instructors.

Puking on The Grinder

My first Marine Corps breakfast was most memorable. In those days, just about everyone smoked, including the majority of my fellow recruits in Platoon 290 and all of the drill instructors. We were marched to a chow hall and told, in very harsh terms, that we had just a very few minutes to go through the line, eat our chow, and be back on the grinder (massive parade ground) in formation. The drill instructor said that the "smoking lamp would be lit" for one cigarette after chow, but only if *every recruit* was back in the minimal time allotted. After the very short time allotted, all but one recruit was in the formation, and that one person was about 30 seconds late. Consequently, that one late recruit was the only person allowed to have a cigarette, but had to simultaneously smoke a cigarette from each of the smokers in the platoon. Every recruit who smoked gave the late recruit a cigarette, and the whole group of cigarettes was placed in his mouth and lit, and then a bucket was placed over his head. Then the drill instructor ordered the poor fellow to "smoke, smoke, smoke, inhale more, inhale more, etc." Finally the kid puked his guts out, with the bucket still over his head. What a pathetic sight, and something that I can still easily visualize. I don't think I have ever visited MCRD in the past 50 years, since I was in boot camp, without looking at about the exact spot where that incident occurred, and thinking about that first USMC breakfast.

Meeting Our Drill Instructors

We were "introduced" to our drill instructors right after morning chow on the first day. Our greeting consisted of more yelling and screaming than I had ever heard in one place, and degrees of obsessive profanity that exceeded anything that I had ever heard. The senior drill instructor was Staff Sergeant Clements and the two junior drill instructors were Sergeants Bridler and Esputo. I cannot think of anything that these people did not criticize, and virtually nothing – not even our mothers – were immune from their hostile and vulgar comments. We were continually told that, "We were lower than whale shit, and that was found at the bottom of the ocean!" With my years of knowledge about the military, I was not the least bit irritated or offended, as I saw this performance for exactly what it was, part of the process to break down the "cheap civilian shit," and build us into United States Marines. Now, over fifty years later, and in a society where political correctness has taken on obsessive levels, I still look back on those days in a positive vein and am not troubled by the manner in which we were treated.

The ranks of the drill instructors are worthy of brief mention, because of the rank and pay grade changes that were taking place in the Department of Defense at the time. Clements was a regular staff sergeant with the pay-grade of E-6, and had crossed rifles displayed on his chevrons. Bridler and Esputo, however, were sergeant E-4, with no crossed rifles in their chevrons, and obviously anxious to be promoted to the permanent rank of sergeant E-5, which would consist of crossed rifles being added to their chevrons. Bridler and Esputo were eventually promoted, but their good fortune was short-lived.

Candy Bar in the Palm Tree

Sweets of any sort were not just available in boot camp, where every minute of the 16-18 hour day was scheduled. About half way through boot camp, my platoon (Platoon 290) got the weeklong night duty to completely clean, (to include sweeping and swabbing the decks), the two- story headquarters of the Second Recruit Training Battalion. On the first night, I saw that there was a candy machine, but we were threatened with horrible things if we even looked at that machine, let along got anything out of it.

Nevertheless, the next night I took a dime (from my locker box) with me and, when no one was looking, bought a Mounds candy bar. I concealed it and when we returned to our Quonset hut, after "taps," I snuck into a darkened area and took one heavenly bite; boy did it taste good. I then wrapped it up, crawled up a palm tree, and hid my treasure. I made it last for three or four days, and each night climbed up that tree and took another bite. I would have been in big trouble if my sin had been detected.

Every time I visit the Marine Corps Recruit Depot, I look over to where that tree and my Quonset hut had been, and reflect on that Mounds bar. The tree and Quonset hut are long gone, but I can still pretty much identify the exact site.

Drill Instructors Relieved For "Thumping"

A tragedy struck our platoon at about the fourth week of training: our three drill instructors were relieved from duty! We later learned that a recruit from their previous platoon made allegations of brutal treatment in the form of "thumping" (striking a recruit), and the allegations were confirmed by a follow up investigation consisting of interviews with other members of that former platoon. While cursory, we were all asked about any thumping in our platoon, and none of my fellow recruits (to my knowledge) said anything derogatory about Clements, Bridler, or Esputo. We learned that all three were reduced ("busted") in rank and relieved as drill instructors. While they were not with our platoon that long, I perceived them as good and decent men who were trying their best to "mold Marines," and was saddened at their misfortune. Just before graduation, I saw Bridler in a mess hall in a cook's uniform, with a corporal insignia attached to his hat – guess food services must have been his primary military specialty).

While there is no way that I would have reported the incident, I was "thumped" by Staff Sergeant Clements. Subsequent to a field day (obsessive cleaning!) of our Quonset Hut, where cleaning the oil stove was my responsibility, Clements reached way up into the bowels of the stove and his white glove covered hand emerged with a small smudge on the tip of one of his finger! With a clenched fist, he punched me in the stomached for the soiled glove. I just winced, took it like a man, and accepted it as the way the USMC did business – no biggie.

Met New Drill Instructors

If such were possible, our three new drill instructors were even more hostile than the ones they replaced! While not true, and they knew it, they accused my platoon of badmouthing the drill instructors that were relieved, thus contributing to the tragic investigation. The senior drill instructor was Staff Sergeant (E-6) Rawlings, a World War II and Korean War vet who was older than most, and obviously a southerner of some sort. The first of the two junior drill instructors was a big black man, Staff Sergeant (E-5) Jennings, who tried hard to be mean and tough but in reality was a very kind and decent man. The second junior drill instructor was Corporal (E-4) Carlton, whose persona (appropriately so) was that of a mean asshole. It was obvious that they were an able and strong team and, despite my "lower than whale shit" status, I developed a professional affection for all three of them.

Marine Corps Brainwashing – For Duty and Honor

For someone who has not experienced Marine Corps recruit training, this situation may seem hard to believe, but it is absolutely true, and the actions of all concerned are pretty typical given the circumstances. Miller was a squad leader and Shapiro was in that squad, and was Miller's best friend. When tasked with doing a "field day" (obsessive cleaning) on the battalion headquarters building, Miller observed Shapiro buying a candy bar from the vending machine, which was pretty much a mortal sin (as indicated in the previous paragraph, I didn't get caught when I committed the same sin). This situation tore Miller apart because he knew that he had no alternative but to report the actions of his best friend, and knowing full well that the consequences for Shapiro would be pretty harsh. Shapiro understood that as well, and did not fault or criticize Miller for what he had to do. Without exception, all of the other recruits who were present also accepted that Miller had no alternative. These actions were the consequence of the industrial-grade dose of duty and honor that recruits receive during basic training. If Miller had remained silent, the drill instructors would never have known about Shapiro's transgression, but Miller was doing exactly what was expected of him and anything less was not an option. It is this type of training and commitment that sets Marines apart from others. As I recall, Shapiro's penalty involved multiple laps around the several-mile grinder with a field marching pack full of rocks; we all felt he got off easy. Glad I didn't get caught when I did the same thing!

Does Anyone Other than Bushey Know the Answer

The obsession I had with all of the military services, but primarily the Marine Corps, started paying off the day that I entered boot camp. Without exaggerating, I knew everything! While obviously 100 percent focused on all that we were taught, I could have slept through just about every class and still "aced" any exam given. This is not to say that boot camp was a cakewalk, because it was truly tough; unbelievably physically demanding, harsh treatment by the drill instructors (it was an appropriate role they were playing, and I understood that), hand-to-hand combat and other physical skills far beyond physical conditioning, hours of "snapping in" and firing the M-1 rifle, homesickness, etc. Boot camp is intended to be a difficult experience, and it was; but less so for me because I knew so much, knew what to expect in terms of treatment, and would rather have been at MCRD than Disneyland.

"Grab An Eye, Grab A Ball – Kill! Kill! Kill!"

Instilling an aggressive combative spirit in young men is an absolutely essential ingredient in the making of a Marine. Some kids enter the Corps with a background of many fistfights, and others have never raised their fists in anger; I was somewhere in between. While we don't want our young Marines to become physical bullies, we must mold them in a way where they will not retreat from a fight, but rather will seize both the physical and psychological advantage in combative situations. Part of this development took place in a massive sand pit, where hand-to-hand combat was taught. I will never forget the blood-curdling screams of the instructors who taught the recruits, in combat, to, "Grab an eye, grab a ball, kill, kill, kill!" These people sure got my attention, contributed to my aggressiveness (when required), and left me with an expression that I have never forgotten.

The Tragic Overload of a Recruit

This was a sad situation that I watched unfold over a period of a couple of weeks. One of the recruits from Chicago, Private Kaskowitz (pseudonym) became psychologically overloaded with the stress of boot camp. Marine Corps recruit training is tough, with an overabundance of yelling, demands for near-impossible performance, considerable multi-tasking, and stress. Poor

Kaskowitz just couldn't handle it, and was often in some type of a haze; the harder the drill instructors pushed, the more he bogged down. I will never forget a situation where we were being taught to use our new ink stencil kits in the marking of all of our uniforms with our names; Kaskowitz and most of his uniform items were covered with permanent black ink in all the wrong places, with some of his uniform completely ruined by the ink. I can still see that confused young man sitting there in the midst of his mistakes and all the inky mess. Shortly thereafter, in the middle of the night, Kaskowitz dove head first off his top bunk onto the concrete floor, in what I assumed with a suicide attempt. He was rushed to the hospital with what certainly appeared to be severe head trauma, and we never saw him again. At the time, we all thought that Kaskowitz was just a useless "shitbird," but I can now look back and see a young man who, through no fault of his own, absolutely did not have the ability to perform the difficult and unique tasks associated with recruit training.

Enroute and Arrival at Rifle Range

From the establishment of the Marine Corps Recruit Depot in 1919 until 1964, all marksmanship training was conducted at the Camp Matthews rifle range in the hills east of La Jolla, which had been a remote area. The camp was named in honor of one of the Marine Corps' most famous shooters, Brigadier General Calvin B. Matthews. The recruits spent the 6th, 7th, and 8th weeks of boot camp at Camp Matthews. To get there, we were transported in "cattle cars" (military transport vehicles) to a swampy area north of the recruit depot, and then marched through about 10 miles of remote terrain to get to Camp Matthews. When the marksmanship phase of boot camp was over, we were returned to the Recruit Depot by reversing the process. The "swampy area" is now known as Mission Bay, and I doubt that there is a single vacant lot along that 1961 remote terrain.

Everly Brothers at Camp Matthews

Don and Phil Everly were in boot camp at the same time as I was there. I was probably a week or two ahead of them. They were in a series (four platoons) a week or so behind my platoon, but we had some joint training. I will never forget either Christmas Day of 1961 or New Years Day of 1962 (it was one of those), when all of the recruits at the Camp Matthews Rifle Range were taken off the "snapping in" field for an hour or so, taken into a large Butler Hut (kind of like a Quonset Hut on steroids), and treated to a performance of the Everly Brothers. Don and Phil, recruits just like the rest of us (they were reservists, to be released from active duty after six months, then expected to serve another six years in the reserves), sang a bunch of their popular songs (they were BIG entertainers with a number of top songs, such as "Wake Up Little Suzie," "All I Have To Do Is Dream," and "Cathy's Clown," among others). There was no music, just their singing. It was quite a treat, but back to "snapping in" after about an hour. Years later, when we became close friends, Phil Everly told me that this was a very memorable experience for him and Don.

I also remember seeing them on visiting day shortly before all of us graduated. Some very pretty girls visited them. That was OK with me because I was in heaven drinking the cola and eating the fried chicken and chocolate cake my Mom brought down. That meal, after weeks of being deprived of what I really liked to eat, was about as close to heaven as a person could get.

Phil Everly and I later became close friends. When I took over as the commanding officer of Communications Division, two of the police service representatives (dispatchers) were Patti Arnold and Cathy Trischuk (now Cathy Bushey), and they were the best of friends. One day, after Cathy and I were married, she told me that Patti was dating Phil Everly, and I told her we had been in boot camp together. At first she did not believe me, so I wrote a note for Patti to give to Phil, and it referred to their singing in the Butler Hut at Camp Matthews. When he got the note, Phil called me right away and we had a nice conversation. After that, Cathy and I visited him and Patti (both before and after they were married) at their home in North Hollywood, had a fun weekend in Catalina, attended several of their performances (he and Don) in Las Vegas, and a attended a few other functions in their home.

Patti was Phil's third or fourth wife, and they appeared to have a nice marriage. Phil and I would kid each other that with each wife his houses got smaller. Phil and Patty moved to Tennessee, and it was hoped that we would all be able to get together again, however that was not to be. Phil died in early 2014. RIP Marine.

Peeing Through a Tent Opening – Bad Idea!

All of the recruits were housed in eight-men squad tents. The heads (bathrooms) were in a row of wooden structures several hundred feet away. Fortunately, young men have pretty strong bladders and do not usually have to interrupt their sleep to make head calls (like old farts!) However, if it was necessary the recruit had to not only get dressed and walk to the head, but also to first untie the ropes that secured the tent's door. For this reason, some recruits would just pee through the narrow opening between the tent and tent flap, without untying the knots, and then run their boot over the moist ground at reveille to conceal their treachery. The drill instructors knew that some recruits were inclined to this short cut and instructed the fire watch recruits to hit any penis they saw with the night sticks they carried. One night I awoke to the screaming of a fire watch for the sergeant of the guard; he saw a penis that belonged to a young man who was relieving himself, and apparently gave it a pretty good whack with the nightstick.

It was not my tent, but I understand the culprit was easy to locate once the tent flap was untied, as he was bent over in pain. I don't know what sanction the midnight pisser experienced, but it couldn't have been pleasant.

Guard Duty at Camp Matthews (Defining Experience)

My first round of guard duty at the Rifle Range at Camp Matthews had an impact on me that has served me well throughout my life, and continues to this day. Camp Matthews is long gone and is the site of the present University of California, San Diego. In 1961, it was desolate and in the middle of nowhere. Through one night, when my entire platoon had guard duty, different people being assigned to different portions of the camp, I was assigned as the lone sentry at "Mike" Range. I had no flashlight. My instructions were to walk a given route continuously for several hours. It was pitch black out and I was the only human in that area (my only nocturnal "companions" being a lot of coyotes, skunks, etc.). Part of my route was to walk inside and cover the entire length of a long target shed, which was probably 75 to 100 yards long. It was completely dark inside, with rows of rooms on either side of the center walkway, and the whole place creaked with aging wood.

Walking through that dark creaky shed was scary, at first. Upon entering the long center pathway, you could see no light at the other end, but had to just keep walking. After making it about half way through the shed, you could start to see faint moonlight, which was the other end of the shed. By the time that tour of duty was over, I was strutting confidently into that sea of darkness, with my confidence weighing more heavily than my fear. This is classic USMC behavior, bullshit yourself out of fear and into confidence.

Darkness has been my friend ever since that night at Camp Matthews so long ago. Throughout my Marine Corps and law enforcement experiences, I have learned to depend on ambient light, and use a flashlight only as a last resort. Part of this is driven by a continuing desire to see others without being seen myself, and recognizing that artificial light really screws up your night vision.

Staff Sergeant Jennings's Goodness was Obvious

Loved ones were permitted to visit recruits on Sundays once they reaching the rifle range. My parents and brother visited me at Camp Matthews, and it was somewhat emotional because of a bit of homesickness. Although phone calls were not normally permitted, for some reason I got permission to call home that night after the visit. While on the phone with my mom, I clearly had tears in my eyes, and up popped one of the three drill instructors, Staff Sergeant Jennings, just as I hung up. He got in my face and asked if I had been crying, to which I said, "No sir, something got in my eye." He made some remark about the dust in the air and told me to get back to the platoon area. He clearly knew that I had teared up with homesickness. He was a drill instructor and as such knew how to be harsh, but he was a very decent and wonderful man whose qualities of decency and humanity could not be masked by his "Smokey bear" campaign hat.

I ran across Staff Sergeant Jennings a few years later in the PX at Camp Hansen on Okinawa. As I recall, he was in the 9th Motor Transport Battalion. We had a nice chat. I regret never having seen him again.

205 and One Round Left

Talk about pressure. It was important to me that I qualify as no less than a "sharpshooter," which required a score of 210 to 220, with anything above 220, being an "expert." From 190 to 209 was a "marksman," with a medal that looked like and was called "the toilet seat." My brother had always qualified as a "sharpshooter" and I wanted the same medal, which was an attractive Maltese cross, suspended from a bar that contained the word "Sharpshooter." I was on the 500-yard line, shooting prone, with one round remaining and a score of 205. I would need a bull's eye to get that coveted medal. I made it! This was a very happy moment.

That wonderful and coveted USMC sharpshooter medal is the shooting award that I chose to put on the front cover of these memoirs. For the vast majority of my career, ever since transitioning to the M-16, I have consistently shot expert, which is a higher award and represented by a different medal. However, because of how powerful that experience was for me in boot camp, it is the sharpshooter's award that I chose to conspicuously display.

Started to "Pass Out" on the Grinder

My platoon had a shooting award ceremony on the grinder almost immediately after the forced march back to MCRD from Camp Matthews. For whatever reason, perhaps I had unknowingly locked my knees, I was in the process of passing out just as one of the drill instructors, Staff Sergeant Jennings, was walking past me. He immediately recognized what was happening and directed me to a nearby curb in the shade and told me to sit down. Within a couple of minutes, I felt fine and, without being directed to do so, immediately returned to the formation. I think this type of behavior and spirit contributed to my selection as one of the few promotees out of boot camp.

Best Boot Camp Pal Later Killed In Action

There really wasn't much socialization among recruits in boot camp, at least not in the conventional sense. Every waking moment was spent in the performance of various tasks, and there was really very little opportunity for conversation among the recruits. However, to the extent that I had a best buddy in Platoon 290, that best buddy was Private Russell Rowe from Chicago. We stood next to each other in the same squad, had adjacent bunks, and were usually paired up in hand-to-hand combat. Rowe was a good dude and despite our mutual commitment to always stay in touch with each other, I never saw him again after infantry training. In 1965, Russ was killed as the result of machine gun fire from insurgents during a deployment to the Dominican Republic (DomRep). RIP Russ.

M-1 to the M-14 to the M-16 in One Enlistment!

In Boot Camp, we were issued the M-1 rifle, a weapon that was developed early in World War II, and used in that war and also during the Korean Conflict. It was a great weapon and I knew it intimately, having learned to field strip it blindfolded before entering the Corps. Upon graduation from Boot Camp, I kept the rifle that I had been issued and carried it with me to my first duty station, H&S Company, 2nd Battalion, 1st Marine Regiment, 1st Marine Division, Camp Pendleton.

In September of 1962, the month before the Cuban Missile Crisis, we were issued the M-14 rifle (308 caliber with a 20 round magazine). Most of us complained about having lost the M-1 (obviously, we had to turn them in), but in reality the M-14 were most likely superior, especially with the expanded magazine and the ability to fire fully automatic (when issued the adapter to do so). Just before completing my first enlistment, the Marine Corps (Army too) upgraded to the M-16 (7.62 caliber). The M-16 had several models and was used in Vietnam and other places until the late 1990s. Although there were problems in jamming with the early models, much of it no doubt related to maintaining and cleaning the weapon, the M-16 served the military well during the time it was used.

From Loser to Honor Graduate in Three Months

I was the classic "dead end kid" when I entered the Marine Corps. I had quit high school and was working at the MonArc Auto Body Shop in Monrovia. I can't really say that I completed two years of high school, but I was there part of the time for two years. Most of my grades were "D" and "F," with an occasional "C" and maybe even a "B" in something like PE! I was an OK worker at MonArc and other places that I had worked, but certainly nothing special. I think I was basically a good person and was very polite, and was reasonably well liked by people, but my future was not very bright. The only real goal I had in life, and that was an obsessive goal, was to join the Marine Corps on my 17th birthday. Unfortunately, my birthday fell on a Sunday. However all the paperwork had been done, my parents had signed for me in advance, and on Monday, November 13, 1961, I was sworn into the Marine Corps and started my basic training at the Marine Corps Recruit Depot in San Diego. I am fond of telling people that although my body was born in Alhambra, my spirit and true soul were born in San Diego during the period of November 13, 1961 through February 10, 1962. Something sure as hell happened!

The proudest day in my life, and nothing yet has outshined it, was my graduation from boot camp on February 10, 1962. A day or two before graduation I was told that I had been selected as one of the six or seven recruits to be meritoriously promoted to private first class – WOW. I will never forget marching out by the base theatre, past my mom, pop, and brother, with those wonderful PFC stripes on my sleeve. As I type this, I actually started to tear up as I reflected on the significance of that event. Obviously, my family was very proud of me. I was pretty proud of myself.

God bless the Marine Corps. I am one of those lost souls who ended up with a good life, and the Marine Corps is among the major reasons why.

I still recall going into the head on the evening of graduation, as we prepared to ship out the next morning for infantry training at Camp Pendleton. I kept looking at myself in the mirror with those PFC chevrons on my collar. Boy, was I something! The next morning I learned that being a PFC was not as big a deal to some other people as it was to me.

The Left Guide

I did not know what a "left guide" was until I became one. Two or three weeks before graduation, we had the platoon photo taken. All of us were in our winter service green uniforms. The protocol was for the drill instructors and two top recruits, one of whom was the right guide, to be on the front row of bleachers, with the rest of the platoon on the rear benches. As the photographer was positioning everyone, he asked to have the "left guide" seated to the right of the drill instructors, and the "right guide" (who was Edwin Hopkins) seated on their left. To my surprise, I was identified as the "left guide" and told to sit with the drill instructors on the bench. This incident was the first indication that I was doing exceptionally well. I knew I was doing well, but not that well. I still have and treasure this platoon photo. Little did any of us realize that the two recruits seated on either side of the three drill instructors would eventually become commissioned officers, and me a full colonel!

In about 1978, I was a Marine captain on active duty and participating in an exercise at Fort Irwin, out by Barstow, California. I made a run onto the Marine Logistics Base and ran across 2nd Lieutenant Ed Hopkins. He had just been commissioned as a

Limited Duty Officer in contracts administration, and we had a nice chat. When he entered the Marine Corps, he had four years prior service as a Navy corpsman (he had been wounded in Korea) and four additional years of service in the Air Force. At graduation, he had two rows of ribbons and jump wings. Not surprisingly, he was both the platoon and series honor man.

Crossing Paths With Previous Drill Instructors

During my four years of active enlisted service, I ran info four of my six drill instructors. As previously mentioned, I saw Bridler in a mess hall at the San Diego Recruit Depot, where he was assigned as a cook, and had just been busted in rank to corporal. In 1962, while attending the Message Center Course at the Division Schools at Camp Pendleton, I ran across and had a nice discussion with Clements, who then was an ABC (Atomic, Biological, and Chemical) specialist/instructor, with the rank to which he had been busted, sergeant (E-5). In 1963, while in the post exchange at Camp Hansen on Okinawa, I ran into and had a very nice chat with then Sergeant (E-5) Jennings, who was a motor transport NCO in the 9th Motor Transport Battalion. I felt bad for him that he was not able to make the cut for promotion to regular staff sergeant from the previous temporary rank that he held when assigned as a drill instructor. Finally, in 1965, while assigned to the Communications Center at El Toro, I bumped into Carlton, who had been promoted to sergeant and was assigned as a corrections specialist in the brig; we had a nice chat and decided to get together at a later time for lunch; I am saddened that it never occurred. Like most Marines, my drill instructors were very special men who played a major role in my life, and I think about them often. My occasional efforts to contact them have all been in vain.

Chapter Six
2nd INFANTRY TRAINING REGIMENT

In February of 1962, following three months of basic training, I was transferred to the 2nd Infantry Training Regiment, at Camp Pendleton, for one month of training in the tactics and equipment of the Marine infantry battalion. In addition to squad and platoon tactics, the weapons included: browning automatic rifle, .30 caliber machine gun, flame thrower, 3.5 rocket launcher, and additional instruction in the use of hand grenades, booby traps, and explosives. Unfortunately, I was among the unlucky ones selected to spend a couple of extra weeks at the 2nd ITR, as a messman.

Spud Locker Czar

My entire series (four platoons or about 250 new Marines), were taken via "cattle cars" to Camp Pendleton, specifically to Camp San Onofre and the Infantry Training Regiment (ITR) to start a four-week infantry-training course. At ITR, some of the new Marines, including those who had been meritoriously promoted in boot camp, were given temporary ranks for the rolls they would play, and the temporary ranks were reflected by arm bands with the respective stripes (sergeant for squad leader, staff sergeant for platoon leader, etc.). I just knew that I would get one of those coveted temporary training ranks, and would be a top performer in infantry training. Wrong!

The entire company (formed from the four platoons) was in formation when about twenty names were called out, including mine, and those persons were directed to fall in outside the regular company formation. We fell out, and the rest of the company was marched off! This was not a good sign. Then a corporal in a cook's uniform took charge and informed us that we were on "mess duty" for two weeks. This couldn't be happening to me. The corporal told us to stow our gear in the Quonset hut behind us and get over to the mess hall. As the others complied, I approached the corporal and had a conversation that, to this day, I can almost recall verbatim. I very carefully and politely told him that I thought there had probably been a mistake in assigning me to mess duty, because I was a Pfc. He give me a funny look, was silent for a moment or so, and responded: "So you are. Ok, you are in charge of the spud locker. Now put your shit away and get your ass over to the mess hall!"

I can laugh now, but was absolutely devastated by this mess duty. I was ready to start basking in the glory of my new exalted position, hopefully get liberty and go home for the weekend, and perform as a true leader in infantry training. It was long two weeks, reveille at 0245 hours and lights out at 2200 hours, with a few short breaks between meals. I did not get much sleep, but sure as hell peeled a lot of potatoes! After two weeks, I joined "Mike" company for my four weeks of infantry training, got and wore my coveted temporary training rank (sergeant-squad leader), graduated, and went home on my ten-day boot camp leave. As of 2012, the old mess hall is now a fitness center and the little hut that was the spud locker is gone, but the foundation still exists; I occasionally visit that foundation and reflect on that experience.

BBs for a Trained Killer

I came home to Duarte on my boot camp leave. It was most enjoyable, especially hanging out around the high school after classes got out, and letting everybody see the loser that made good. Naturally, I did the obligatory visit to the high school, strutting around in my dress green Marine Corps uniform. After a couple of days, I got a little bored with what to do with myself until school let out. I had an idea: shoot my beloved BB gun at cans in the back yard. Unfortunately, I was out of BBs so I drove to Reagan's Toy Store (later the space became part of the Bank of America in Duarte) to get some. I told the women I wanted two containers of BBs. She promptly put them on the counter, but surprised me by asking for my identification. I proudly whipped out my Marine Corps I.D. card and, after looking at it, she said that I was only seventeen years old (true), and the law said you could not by BBs unless you were eighteen (also true). I replied that I was a United States Marine, a "trained killer," and that I felt that I should be able to by BBs! She responded with something I will never forget: "You may be a trained killer, but you are going to have to come back with your mother if you want those BBs!"

I was furious and humiliated. When I told my mom and pop of the conversation, they laughed themselves silly, but at the time I failed to see the humor. I certainly see the humor now, and it is one of my favorite stories.

Chapter Seven
SECOND BATTALION, FIRST MARINE REGIMENT (2/1)

In late March of 1962, following my six weeks of infantry training and my ten-day boot camp leave, I was assigned to one of the Marine Corps' thirty or so infantry battalions, the 2nd Battalion of the 1st Marine Regiment, located with the other two battalions of the first regiment at Camp San Mateo, which is one of the many smaller bases within Camp Pendleton. The 1st Marine Regiment was one of the three regiments that made up the infantry manpower of the 1st Marine Division at Camp Pendleton. The 2nd Marine Division was at Camp Lejeune in North Carolina, the 3rd Marine Division was scattered throughout Japan and the island of Okinawa, and the 4th Marine Division was made up of reserve units throughout the United States, Hawaii, and Alaska.

"Reporting In" to My First Unit

After boot leave, I reported to the aforementioned battalion, where I was assigned to the Communications Platoon within the Headquarters & Service Company. It was pre-determined that I would be assigned to the message center, no doubt because of my typing ability; I could only type about 8-10 words a minute (if that), but that was breakneck speed compared to others! Most of the other troops could not type at all. I slept in a bunk bed in a large open barracks, along with about 80 other Marines; the corporals and sergeants slept at one end in their own corner surrounded by wall lockers.

Ignorance With Stripes – Liberty Cancelled (Lasting Impression)

I had an experience not long after arriving at 2/1 that left a lasting impression on me, and has influenced my actions in the leadership arena for my entire life. The battalion had just returned from overseas and just about everyone was on leave, and the new folks, such as me, were trickling in each day. There were few officers and staff non-commissioned officers around and the few supervisors were buck sergeants. My boss, for a week or so, was a big man with a small brain and a big chip on his shoulder, and he treated the few of us that worked for him in a pretty shabby manner. The clincher was his mistaken perception that the group of us, collectively, had failed to do some menial task to his satisfaction, and as a result he canceled our weekend liberty.

This really bothered me. I was upset at not being able to go home as I had expected, but concerned and disappointed that someone like this was able to run rampant and mistreat the troops. He was out of control, and playing out his idiosyncrasies at the expense of innocent subordinates who were completely at his mercy. Even though only seventeen, I made a commitment to myself, then and there that I would never allow someone to behave this way if I ever found myself in a position of authority. I have often reflected on that situation throughout my life as a leader, and strongly encourage others to take measures to prevent troublesome subordinates from mistreating their troops/ employees. Probably not a good analogy, but I don't think you can blame a dog for chasing someone when the real problem is the person who lets that dog run loose.

Message Center School

A couple of months after reporting into 2/1, we new folks were sent to various schools to be trained in our assigned military occupational specialties (MOS's). Again, no doubt because I was able to type (barely), I was selected for Message Center School, which was located in the Horno Area of Camp Pendleton. This was a three-week academic course, and I graduated 7th out of about 25 Marines. Pretty good for a high school dropout!

My typing skills are worthy of brief discussion. In high school, during my occasional visits (!), included a year or so of typing classes, I obviously learned something and gained some skills. My mom really pushed me to take typing classes, and said it was a skill that would always be of benefit throughout my life. Thanks mom, you were right!

I continue to see myself as a combat infantry Marine (an old beat-up and useless one at this advanced stage in my life!), but remember a number of times when the grunts in my battalion (those with the hard core infantry MOS's) were crawling in mud and I was sitting in a comfortable communications center. Let there be no doubt, I spent plenty of time in the mud, but a little less because of my MOS. Thanks again, mom!

Go Fetch An ST-One and a TR-Double E – Now!

In Marine Corps Communications, even to this day, each piece of "Comm Gear" has a two or three letter designation, followed by two or three numbers. The field phone of that era was the EE-8, the switchboard was SB-22, the primary tactical radios were the PRC-10 and PRC-25, etc. This type of designation referred to every piece of gear. New Marines in the Communications field were often sent all over the base to find a couple of critical pieces of equipment, such as the ST-1 and the TR- Double E. With each place they tried unsuccessfully, a more tenured Marine would send them to some other location. It usually took them a couple of hours before figuring out that these designations were for a stone and a tree! There are different types of wire used in communications, and unsuspecting young Marines would sometime be directed to locate shoreline as well!

The Grand Daddy of All Hangovers!

My first hangover had to be the worst as well. I was about 17½ and assigned one night to the graveyard shift in the Message Center at Camp San Mateo. After getting off work at about 0800, and knowing it was just about impossible to sleep in the barracks with all the noise, I drove to San Clemente Beach and tried to get some sleep - not a good idea because I baked in the sun and probably got somewhat dehydrated.

About 1800 I joined a few of my buddies in an abandoned Quonset hut for a birthday party for one of my pals. For dinner, I had a couple of pieces of the birthday cake. Then I started drinking, and did I ever! I drank considerable quantities of whiskey, bourbon, peppermint schnapps, gin, and vodka; very stupid but I didn't know anything about drinking and certainly did not understand the horrible consequences of mixing the booze. I can still remember being drunk and driving my car back to the barracks, and lying in my bunk as the world around me revolved.

When I woke up the next morning at reveille, I was still drunk, but decided to go to the mess hall and get something to eat. At the mess hall, all I really cared for was milk, which ultimately just curdled in my stomach. I started puking at about 1100 and kept puking for about two days! In those days, due to what I believe was a smaller than usual esophagus, vomiting was difficult and painful and usually took me to my knees, which just made things all the worse. I went into the comm center between puking bouts to create the illusion that I was working. On Friday I had liberty, but had to invite one of my pals to come home with me because I was still too sick to even drive my car. On the way home, I still remember having to open the door and puke in the street during one stop for a signal. This had to be the mother of all hangovers!

Bravado on a Walkway in Duarte

One evening, while home on liberty, I was in my "greens" (winter service alpha uniform) and walking along the walkway of the shopping center in Duarte (the only one). A group of four or five men were walking my way and it did not appear that they were inclined to move for me and I damn sure was not going to move for them. As a result, I just bumped my way through them with bravado (and stupidity!) One of them asked me to stop, said he had been a Marine and told me I was acting in a way that would get my "ass kicked!" I pretty much kissed him off and continued on my way. The guy was right and there is no doubt that four or five men could have done some real damage. This was a good example of the bravado and confidence that the Corps instills in young men. Quite a change in the demeanor from someone who was just a high school loser less than six months prior.

Passing The G.E.D. Examination!

Not long after graduating from Message Center School, I signed up to take the GED Examination (General Education Development Equivalent – accepted as high school graduation). It was administered in an old WWII building at "Mainside" (this described most of the buildings at Camp Pendleton, as WWII had not been that long before). I passed on the first try! I still don't know how I could have passed; I was a horrible student and seldom attended school. I guess something must have stuck! Maybe I sat next to someone who wrote big?

Barracks and Open Squad Bays

The vast majority of today's service personnel sleep in rooms with not more than three other people, and usually less. In my enlisted era, those below the rank of staff sergeant slept in barracks with open squad bays; a massive room with metal racks (bunk beds), typically occupied by 60-80 men, with a large communal bathroom, containing sinks and showers, at one end. Privacy was non-existent. In most instances, non-commissioned officers (corporals and sergeants) would have single racks in a corner of the squad bay that was separated from the lance corporals and below by wall lockers. While I would certainly have liked to have had a small room, I must say in retrospect that the open squad bays most likely contributed in a positive way to the strengthening of social skills and tolerance, which is a good thing because there really were no alternative options; get along with others or horrible things would occur!

Rifle Racks in the Open Squad Bays

In today's military, all weapons, including rifles and pistols, are closely controlled and stored in a secured armory when not in actual use. This is a far cry from how rifles and pistols were "secured" in my era. Rifles were kept in a rifle rack in the center of the open squad bay, and most often individually secured with the assigned Marine's combination lock, and it was not unusual for one or two of the rifles in the rack of twenty or so to be completely unsecured. Pistols were typically stored in an armory, but it was not unusual for them to occasionally be kept in the wall locker of the Marine to whom it was issued. While I am sure that it occurred, I do not personally recall the theft of an individual weapon during that era. Unlike today, it was also a common practice in those days for Marines to retain the same weapon when they changed commands, which meant taking it with them, with security precautions, as they traveled to their new command. When I graduated from recruit training, I took my M-1 Garand with me to my first duty station, and kept it until issued the M-14 in September of 1962.

While unheard of today, I actually took my rifle on liberty one time. As a PFC, I put my M-1 in my car when I went home one weekend and, with rounds that I had retained from my recent qualification, took the rifle to the Fish Canyon Shooting Range above the city of Duarte and did some shooting, along with one of my civilian pals. It was not an authorized thing to do, but the sanction would not have been much had my activities come to someone's attention. Just a different era.

Lance Corporal Anderson's "Stretching Exercises"

The occasionally tendency of virile young men to occasionally find relief for their sexual urges in a self-imposed way is one of those life realities that is seldom discussed. However, when such a desire reaches crisis proportions in the middle of the night while in bed, while in a barracks, the only option is to seek relief in a way that might be obvious to some of the other 60-80 young men in that intimate little open squad bay, because of old rickety and squeaky two-man racks (bunk beds). At one time there was a pretty decent fellow named George who had the top bunk while I had the bottom bunk in our two-man cozy arrangement. While I understood George's occasional spontaneous lust, his urges came on at the worst times, and often when I was sleeping the soundest. The squeaking and vibrations that stemmed from his manual manipulations, with our WWII era racks, interfered with my sleep and became a sore spot in our relationship. When I raised the issue, always gently, he attributed the machinations to his "stretching" exercises. Despite my suggestions that he find other times and locations for his "stretching exercises," his disruptive one-person lust continued until his success solved the problem for both of us; he promoted to corporal and got a single bunk behind the row of wall lockers in the coveted "NCO quarters."

I have always wished that I had the ability to draw, and have been envious of those folks who draw caricatures and creative images of funny situations. Just imagine how much fun a talented cartoonist could have with a pissed-off private first class and a lust-driven lance corporal doing his "stretching exercises" in a rickety bunk bed!

As I reflect on this situation, I have to acknowledge that George was probably not the only young man to lie in a lonely bed and think about the girl back home. Had bells been attached to each of the racks, at about midnight the squad bay would probably have sounded like the Washington Cathedral at high noon on Easter Sunday!

"Halt, Who Goes There?" - As I Bounced Down the Hill!

This was both a funny and very critical lesson as well. My battalion was involved in a field exercise in the Case Springs area of Camp Pendleton. Another PFC, "Alf" Anderson (great guy, actually from Sweden) and I were assigned a critical post for 50 percent command post security, which meant that one of us always had to be awake and vigilant to prevent a penetration by the "opposing forces." During one of my tours it was pretty cold so I decided to drape my sleeping bag over my shoulders, then I decided to sit down, then I decided to just lay down and listen – while not intentional, I fell asleep. The next thing I knew I was being dragged down the hill by the very opposing forces I was supposed to be alert for. I still recall yelling out, "Halt Who Goes There!" as I was being dragged down that hill in my sleeping bag! We appropriately got reamed for not remaining alert, and were both required to stay awake for the rest of the night. That was a good lesson and I don't believe I ever fell asleep again when assigned to perimeter security.

Two New Second Lieutenants from the Naval Academy

My first experience with officers who were Naval Academy graduates took place in mid-1962, when two brand new second lieutenants reported into the battalion. They had just completed The Basic School (TBS), the first step for officers after commissioning, and 2/1 was their first assignment. Talk about a contrast, one of them was the epitome of professionalism and the other was a shitbird. Lieutenant Jolley really had his act together, had a solid professional demeanor, and gained almost instant credibility. The other, whose name I do not recall, was obviously intelligent, but looked like "Sad Sack" in his uniform and spent some time hanging out with the enlisted troops, traits that officers just did not display. Jolley deployed with the battalion to Okinawa, but the other fellow pretty much disappeared and most likely was separated from the Marine Corps (perhaps claiming to be a conscientious objector, or something of that nature).

Teletype Machines – Useless in the Field

My primary military occupational specialty (MOS) was message center man. In an infantry battalion, the Message Center is an absolute key to the command element and the entity involving all incoming and outgoing message traffic. The key piece of equipment was the Teletype machine, which worked reasonably well in a garrison/fixed location, but were a pain in the ass in the field. Because of frequent redeployments and the numerous components that made up the field Teletype systems, these systems were just more trouble than they were worth in the field. During fast-moving operations involving numerous field relocations we often found excuses to use runners and other means of passing message traffic. Thank goodness our military folks now have such great equipment, as opposed to the WWII and Korea vintage stuff that was the mainstay during my enlisted days.

Corporal Mangan Gets a "Hot Foot"

One of the "old salts" in the Battalion, Corporal Mangan, after a hard night of drinking, frequently slipped into a storage area and went to sleep during the day. One afternoon, a couple of his "old salt" buddies rigged up a contraption of cardboard and matchbooks, carefully and quietly attached it to one of his boots, ignited it, and stood back to watch the action. The device erupted into flames and essentially cooked the boot it was attached to. The boot obviously got very hot, and eventually the very hot boot started burning his foot. He flew off the table he had been sleeping on, yelling and screaming every profanity imaginable, "hotfooting" it around the communications warehouse, and was truly in a blind rage; there was no way to quickly get the hot laced-up combat boot off his foot. His buddies were rolling in the aisles. It was an ugly, but very funny spectacle. I was a new kid, and it was not in my best interests to laugh, but it was hard not to!

PFC Bushey and the Rendezvous Ballroom

What a great place! This historic structure built in 1928 and then rebuilt in 1935 after it first burned down, was a place where all the big bands played beginning in the 1920s and continuing through the 1950s. It was a gigantic structure that stretched from one block to another right on the beachside sand in Balboa. By the 1960s, all the "Surf Music" giants (Beach Boys, Jan and Dean, etc.) were playing there, along with scores of other groups and individuals representing the music of that era. Looking snappy in my tropical USMC uniform, I went there several times on liberty and really enjoyed the music and the girls. Unfortunately, as a "wet-behind-the-ears" and somewhat immature (with respect to the opposite sex) seventeen-year old, I lacked the skills to fully take advantage of the many opportunities that existed. Still, I had a great time. This wonderful landmark, then located directly behind the gift shop on the main drag of the Balboa Peninsula, burned to the ground in 1966. What a terrible loss for generations of young persons who had such good times there and have such wonderful memories of the place.

Pupu Uele and the Trunk Full of Brass

One of the staff sergeants in the Communications Platoon was Pupu Uele, a big Samoan who was the wire section chief. He was not very smart, but a kind man, and his Samoan accent was very strong. He was not very officious, got along pretty well with the lower-ranking guys, and was the only staff sergeant that I recall who allowed enlisted men to address him by his first name.

One day, the whole base was shut down for a search of every inch of Camp Pendleton. As I recall, a case of hand grenades has been stolen and there was an understandably strong effort to find and retrieve them before they left the base. The search was to include personal vehicles as well. This was a problem for me because I had a truck full of empty brass M-1 shell casings that I took from a trashcan on a nearby rifle range; my brother was a re-loading enthusiast and I got them for him. Even though empty and discarded, this brass was not to be taken from the ranges.

All of us with our own vehicles were directed to stand by our cars and be prepared for the big search. My car was a white 1952 Ford Crestline Victoria with "tuck and roll" upholstery and a bongo drum in the rear window. A group of staff non-commissioned officers were walking our way, and Staff Sergeant Uele was among them. I quickly approached Pupu and said I had some brass in my trunk, did not want to get in trouble, and asked that he be the one to inspect my car. He replied. "for five dollar!" I quickly agreed. When he approached my car and I opened the truck, he saw all the brass and said, "holy shit, ten dollar!" Again, I quickly accepted his offer! I later passed him ten dollars when no one was looking.

The Canteen Cup Caper

This is the first of several stories related to Robert Neman (pseudonym), one of the young Marines that I served with. I have been unsuccessful in trying to think of something nice to say about this guy. He was rude, arrogant, insulting, and successfully specialized in pissing people off. He continually did and said stupid things and had no friends that I was aware of. He was squirrely and slight, and I doubt that he could fight his way out of a paper bag. Every time I see the cartoon of the mouse giving the finger to the elephant, I think of Neman. Get the picture?

One day we had a major inspection, conducted as I recall by the commanding general of the 1st Marine Division. This was a very big deal that everyone had been working for weeks in preparation for. One of the components was the "junk on the bunk" inspection where every Marine had all of his gear laid out, in excruciating order, just right, folds measured to the micro inch, everything shined, pressed, and cleaned, etc., etc. Even the socks and skivvies had to be perfectly marked with each person's name, folded precisely, and organized as if there was a little platoon of socks laying at attention on the bunk. It took hours to assemble these works of art and many people, myself included, had a number of clothing items that we only used for these inspections.

When the inspection party, made up of all of the ranking officers in the chain of command, approached Neman, who like the rest of us was standing at attention at the foot of his rack (metal bunk bed), the general stated, pretty much just going through the motions: "Looks good Marine, got all your gear?" Neman responded: "No Sir!" The whole entourage came to a stop, everyone looked kind of confused, and the general stated that it looked like everything was laid out on his bunk. Neman said that he was missing his canteen cup. The general replied something to the effect: "son, it is right there," and pointed to a canteen cup on Neman's rack. Neman responded. "No sir, that cup belongs to a friend of mine in the first battalion because mine was missing!"

If the looks of the officers in the chain of command and the sergeant major could have killed, Neman would have died then and there! This behavior was unnecessary and beyond stupid. Classic Bob Neman; doing stupid things and pissing people off.

Death of Neman's Parents

It happened one Saturday: Neman was on duty in the Battalion Communication Center, and occasional Teletype traffic was trickling in from higher commands; the Battalion was the end of the line for messages.

A couple of our colleagues created a phony message, allegedly from the Red Cross, advising that Neman's parents had been killed in an automobile accident and asking that he be notified! Neman watched the bogus message come over the wire and understandable became very upset.

I thought then that his colleagues' behavior was sick, and still feel that way. This is an indication of how cruel some Marines can be with their humor.

"I am Going to Transfer to the Air Force!

Bob Neman was continually complaining about the Marine Corps, and to this day I can still hear him say: "I wish I had joined the M----- F------ Air Force!" He was always saying this, especially when upset about something, which was most of the time. A few of us, including me, cooked up a remedy to this problem.

We created a very credible appearing, but completely false, Marine Corps order that announced alleged transfer opportunities to the Air Force. The bogus order described MOS (specialty) imbalances among the military services and listed the criteria by which Marines could transfer to the Air Force. We created an extensive list of requirements, and ensured that Neman met every one of them. The order directed any interested Marine to contact his first sergeant. We then posted the phony notice on the company bulletin board. One of the guys then ran into the barracks and told Neman that his dream had been answered, and that he could now transfer to the Air Force, and told him of the order posted on the bulletin board. In typical Neman form, he said his colleague was full of it, and arrogantly stormed out. Still, the temptation was too much and we knew that Neman would make a beeline to the bulletin board to see if there really was such an order. It was there!

Neman immediately entered the Company Office and asked to see the company first sergeant, who just happened to be there. Neman, in his typical arrogant demeanor, told the first sergeant that he wanted an immediate transfer to the Air Force pursuant to the posted order (which we took off the bulletin as he entered the Company Office!) The shit hit the fan with the first sergeant yelling and screaming, and Neman insisting that there was such an order. They both ended up outside the Company Office and the order that Neman insisted existed was not there, and the yelling and screaming by the first sergeant got even worse, with Neman limping back to the barracks with smoke coming out his rear end! This incident did not improve Neman's already bad disposition. At the time, I thought that this was pretty funny; today I think it is ever funnier!

Slaughter Alley

The stretch of highway that stretched through Camp Pendleton, adjacent to the ocean, between the cities of Oceanside and San Clemente, had a well deserve nickname of "Slaughter Alley." At the time, it was two lanes in each direction, which were separated by nothing more than a double yellow line. There were frequent head-on collisions, often involving servicemen and usually caused by someone who was either intoxicated or fatigued. The mayhem resulting from two cars colliding at high speed was absolutely awful, with gory posters containing such images routinely posted around Camp Pendleton. Thank goodness that this stretch of Interstate 5 is now a divided highway. Portions of the old "Slaughter Alley" are still clearly visible, with a considerable section just south of San Clemente now being a recreational vehicle parking area for the San Clemente State Park beaches, and another section serving as a parking area for cars just outside the Las Pulgas Gate at Camp Pendleton.

Emergency Blood Donation – "Need a Note from Your Parents!"

One morning one of our corpsman ran through the company area frantically calling out a bunch of names for Marines to report to the first sergeant, and I was one of those names. It seems that there had been a terrible traffic accident in Oceanside and there was an immediate need for blood of a certain type. This is when I first learned that my blood type of "O" negative was highly sought after for donations. There were 10 or 15 of us, and we were rushed in a military truck to a civilian hospital in Oceanside. We were ushered inside but a snag immediately developed for me because I was only seventeen years old and my parents were not available to give permission for me to give blood! The efforts of the sergeant in charge to explain that I now belonged to the government, and no longer to my parents, and that he was in charge of me, fell on deaf ears. The fact that somebody's life was on the line was secondary to a rule that said parental permission was required for a donor beneath the age of 18, and nobody at that hospital had the common sense to apply reality to the situation. PFC Bushey gave no blood that day.

Poop and the Coffee Table

This is really sick! One of the other Marines in my unit had a unique week-end job in Laguna Beach; defecating on the top of a glass coffee table as a prosperous sicko laid beneath the table watching the action! Obviously, all of his buddies (including me) expressed our reservations about this behavior. He responded that he had to poop anyway, and why not make good money by directing his deposits where a generous person could enjoy them. I guess he and his friend must have been pretty pleased with the relationship because the Marine always had a few bucks in his pocket, and the rest of us were usually broke. I think it is fair to say that all of the rest of us had two common thoughts, outrage at this disgraceful behavior and envy that the prosperous sicko had not met one of us first! Postscript: I ran into my pal, the "depositor," about twenty years later and at that time he was a newly commissioned lieutenant, having received a limited duty commission after many years as a staff non-commissioned officer. I wish that I had remembered to remind him of his poopathons in Laguna Beach.

Chapter Eight
THE CUBAN MISSILE CRISIS

"Mounting Out"

On October 19, 1962, a Friday, I entered the Company Office to get my liberty card to start a long weekend that I had earned. As I approached the duty non-commissioned officer, the first sergeant walked over, removed the box of liberty cards, announced that the base had been shut down, and that the Battalion was "mounting out!" My outfit, the Second Battalion of the First Marine Regiment was the "Ready Battalion Landing Team" for the West Coast for October, with field transport packs made up and secured on the back of our racks (other services would call them "bunks"), and the ability to immediately deploy anywhere in the world should a crisis erupt, supposedly on four-hours notice.

I thought this was a practice drill, as we were having practice "mount outs" quite often, and it was usually more of a logistics drill to see if we could get all of the equipment in embarkation boxes within a given period of time. I just knew that "ENDEX" (the end of the exercise) would be sounded at anytime, but that did not occur. All day and into the night, we prepared gear, organized weapons, turned the keys of our personal vehicles over to a representative from the military police, and performed related tasks. All phones were shut down and no one was permitted to call off base. One of the guys snuck off the base and went into San Clemente to bring back some of our pals who often went on their own form of liberty by crawling out a hole in the fence surrounding the base. This shit was starting to look serious! But what is going on in the world where a Marine battalion is immediately needed? The Berlin Airlift was over; Lebanon had settled down; the "Bay of Pigs" had run its tortured course; what's going on now?

We staged on the San Mateo grinder all night, and as the Sun came up we boarded cattle cars for the short trip to the El Toro Marine Corps Air Station, just south of Santa Ana (no longer in existence). As we approached the tarmac, there were U. S. Air Force C-35 jet military transport aircrafts (Boeing 707s) lined up as far as I could see! Now it was *really* looking serious, but we still thought it was an exercise (the young troops did, anyway – the leadership knew it was the real deal). The battalion, with tons of weapons, ammo, and equipment boarded the aircraft and took off. Obviously, the rumors were rampant; where the hell are we going? About an hour into the flight, a young Air Force crewmember came on the intercom and announced that our destination was Guantanamo Bay, Cuba!

This was the international situation where history records that the United States and the Soviet Union were on the brink of a nuclear war, because of the detected presence of Soviet nuclear missiles in Cuba that were aimed at the United States, and the demand of President John F. Kennedy that the missiles be dismantled. American forces were deployed and ready for ground, air, and sea combat, and quarantine was imposed in the waters around Cuba.

Ultimately, the Soviet Premier Nikita Khrushchev ordered the missiles removed, and the two countries moved back from the brink of a global holocaust. By this time, thousands of soldiers, sailors, airmen and Marines had deployed to the Caribbean and were ready to engage in armed combat of every type. My battalion was one of the very few that was actually on the ground in Guantanamo. In mid-December, we returned to the United States on a WWII troop transport, the *USS Bexar* APA 237 (named after a county in Texas). We passed through the Panama Canal and returned to Camp Pendleton just before Christmas of 1962.

Much later, by watching a history movie, I learned that Kennedy gave up something as well, an agreement to remove the United States missiles in Turkey that were aimed at the Soviet Union. Even with the concession of the missiles, I thought that President Kennedy did a good job.

I Still Dislike Fidel Castro – Just a Little Less

I was excited about the prospect of going into combat, but please not this weekend! Through the girlfriend of one of my buddies, I had a date set up with a drop dead beautiful gal that I had been wooing since we were both high school freshman, and it was all set, or so I thought, for that Saturday night. Unfortunately, that was the same night I arrived in Cuba! All of us harbored an intense dislike of Fidel Castro, but my scorn for him was even worse because he deprived me of date I had long sought.

When I got back to the States, my friend informed me that despite the efforts of his girlfriend, the date was never confirmed. A number of years later I learned that the girl had been in a long-time secret relationship with one of the Duarte High athletic coaches, and that I never had the slightest chance of a relationship with her. The Cuban

Missile Crisis did not cost me a date with that young woman after all. I still dislike Fidel Castro, but just a little less than before.

This Beer Does Not Taste Right!

Upon arrival in Guantanamo Bay, at the onset of the Cuban Missile Crisis, my company was briefly staged on an asphalt grinder outside the enlisted club. We all sat there for an hour or so, and were permitted to have beer. As I drank my beer, it tasted a little odd, but I kept drinking it anyway. As we were told to board the trucks for transit to the base perimeter, I took one last long swallow on my beer to finish it off. That is when I realized that other Marines had mistaken my bottle for an ashtray! About half the ashes and cigarette butts went down my throat. Not a pleasant experience!

Mosquitoes & Hysteria (Defining Experience in my Life)

The flight from California to Cuba took about five hours, and the planes landed at the airfield on the leeward side of the base. It was hotter than hell, about 109 degrees in the shade, and there wasn't any. The humidity had to be close to 100 percent and was so thick you could cut it with a knife. This was the first time in my life, but far from the last, where I experienced heat and humidity so stifling as to be near paralyzing; a reality that I later endured in many other "garden spots" to which I was sent while a Marine. We were issued live ammunition and rushed, via trucks, to the jungles on the other side of the installation, but still within the base, where Navy Seabees were deployed along the fence line (miles and miles long) in an effort to minimize the infiltration of Cuban Army soldiers.

The battalion entered and set up operations in what had to be one of the worst places on earth. The nastiest jungle imaginable with stale waters everywhere (it rained on and off all the time), more critters of every type than I had ever seen, unbelievably thick foliage and mosquitoes - millions of hungry and pissed-off mosquitoes! Due to our rapid deployment, there were many things that none of us had with us, and there were no mosquito repellant or mosquito nets, nor was there any likelihood of obtaining such items within the next day or so!

This was initially, for a few minutes, the absolute worst time in my life up until then. All of us were sustaining non-stop, multiple mosquito bites on every exposed part of our bodies, which meant face, neck, arms, and hands. I was swatting and swatting and swatting, and naturally my efforts were making no difference; the hand that I was swatting with had just as many mosquitoes clinging to it as the arm I was trying to get the mosquitoes off!

I was starting to panic and was literally on the verge of hysteria, and then something in my mind snapped. I settled down, became calm and recall, as if it were yesterday, saying "fuck it, help yourself, there is enough blood for all of us!" This was among the most significant events in my life, a necessary mindset that proved essential in Cuba and other places where Marines go. I was pleased and proud of myself and knew that something very special had just happened in those previous few minutes.

Commandant Visits the Troops in the Field

Within several days of arriving in Cuba, General David M. Shoup, then Commandant of the Marine Corps, visited our field command post. I was among the gaggle of Marines who gathered around him as he said whatever he said, probably something about him being proud of us, upholding the traditions of the Corps, importance of the mission, etc. My great recollection is what I thought then, and continue to think now of the foolish appearance of his uniform. He wore utilities, but over each breast pocket was a red patch with gold lettering and a gold trim. One patch indicated USMC (or Marines?) and the other SHOUP (OR CMC?) I thought it was unnecessarily flashy and not very Marine Corps. At the time I was a private first class. I could not have imagined that the next time I would have a conversation with a commandant in the field that I would be a full colonel and the primary briefer.

Bushey Reports to the Sergeant Major – "You Are Only 17!"

A few days after arriving in Cuba, I was out stringing comm' wire when another Marine chased me down and said that I was to immediately report to the battalion sergeant major! He was equal to the lord in rank pecking order and I was apprehensive of why he called for PFC Bushey. When I got to his office (sitting behind an embarkation box in a tent), he informed me that I should not have been allowed to deploy to Cuba, because I was only 17 years old, and that Marine Corps orders prohibited anyone from serving in a combat zone until they had reached the ripe old age of 18!

He told me to get my gear, as I was being returned the United States immediately. I did not think Cuba was a good place, and like everyone else I was frightened (by now we knew of the potential missile holocaust), but the thought of being jerked out of my platoon and away from my fellow Marines, and being removed because of my age was devastating.

I came as close as I ever had to begging. I told the sergeant major that I joined the Marine Corps to serve my county, to fight, and to die if necessary. I told him that I would feel disgraced if removed, and talked about my training, my skills, and how my departure would create a loss in my section (that was a bit of an exaggeration!) I pleaded with him to not send me home. I reminded him that I was only two or three weeks away from turning eighteen.

I don't recall his exact words, but the sergeant major replied with something pretty close to the following: "Son, I am a sergeant major in the United States Marine Corps and my job is to ensure that orders are carried out, two days or two weeks makes no difference, the bottom line is that you cannot be in a combat zone as a 17 year old, period!" He paused, appeared to be reflecting, then continued: "Right now, however, I am up to my ass in alligators and am having trouble getting all this shit on my plate out of the way. You issue is pretty close to the bottom of the stack and will probably take two or three weeks before I can get to it. Get your ass back to your platoon for the time being!" He then looked me right in the eyes with somewhat of a mischievous twinkle in his, and a slight smile on his wrinkled face. I thanked him profusely; he nodded slightly and went back to work. I never heard another word about the issue and turned eighteen a couple of weeks later.

I later learned that he also joined the Marine Corps as soon as he turned seventeen, and saw extensive combat in several World War II Pacific campaigns before turning eighteen.

Weapon Misfires in Guantanamo – Thank God!

This was a very bad situation that had the extremely real potential to not only be a fork in my road, but could easily have been the *end* of my road had it not been for an inexplicable weapon malfunction. In a logic which, even after all these years, continues to escape me, my brother convinced my parents to purchase and send a handgun to me in Cuba, but the damn thing was a single-shot .22 caliber Derringer. I think it likely that my brother wanted one so he convinced my mom to buy the matched set; he got one and the other was mailed in a plain package to me in Cuba, with a few loose bullets. When I opened the package and read the letter, I also placed a round in the chamber.

At that time one of my buddies, clearly not rocket scientist material, grabbed it, proclaimed it to be a toy, cocked the hammer, and pointed right at me! I pleaded with him to put it down and insisted that it was loaded and that it was not a toy, at which time he pulled the trigger! Thank God, it did not fire; it turned out to be a manufacturing defect where the hammer spring was not strong enough to cause the rim fire cartridge to fire. I could not believe that I was still alive and had been so lucky; somebody had to be watching over me that day. I can only imagine the consequences had I sustained a fatal wound; my parents and brother would have experienced degrees of sadness and guilt that I believe would have triggered the beginning of the end of their lives.

Don't Let Dorman Kill the Lieutenant!

Upon the arrival of my battalion in Cuba, the Communications Platoon got a new commander, 2nd Lt. Paul G. Davens (pseudonym). He was an OK person, but very *gung ho* and clearly in love with himself. Because of the remnants of a very recently removed and somewhat conspicuous officer candidate school patch, it was clear that he had not been an officer very long, but he acted like an old salt who knew everything there was to know about the Corps and the art of leadership; truly, he was lean on both counts. Worse, he wore a Ruger .357 old western style revolver in a custom holster, as opposed to the government-issued .45 semi-automatic pistols; he also sported a large handlebar moustache. I am aware that he later developed into a fine officer, but he was pretty much a laughable dork while our boss in Cuba.

One of the truly old time Marines in our platoon was a "retread" Corporal whose name was Bennie Dorman (pseudonym), who had previous seen combat in Korea and who had returned to the Corps after a few years stint in CivDiv (we sometimes called civilian life "civilian division.") Dorman had no use for Davens and one night when drunk actually threatened to kill the lieutenant, which most of us saw as just the stupid remarks of a drunk and nothing to be taken seriously. Lieutenant Davens *did* take the remark seriously, however, and directed the communications chief, SSgt Aretakis (RIP) to assign a man to guard the lieutenant while he slept in his hammock in the jungle. I still recall the guidance that Aretakis gave to the men that kept a vigil over the sleeping lieutenant, "Don't let Dorman kill the lieutenant!"

While attending the Command & Staff College at Quantico, when I was a lieutenant colonel in the early 1990s, I ran across an article in a professional journal written by Colonel Paul G. Davens. I managed to locate him: at the time, he was finishing his career as the top Marine at a Navy-Marine Corps ROTC unit at an eastern university. He was very gracious and we had a nice chat, and it was clear that he had long overcome his not untypical, newly-commissioned foolish behavior, and went on to a very successful Marine Corps career. We reminisced about our service in Cuba, but having to guard him from Corporal Dorman was not among the issues that we discussed.

Torn Hands and Comm Wire

Although my military specialty was message center, I spent a great deal of my time in Cuba working as a field wireman. We laid miles and miles of comm' wire, which was necessary in order to have communications between the various units, and especially out to the isolated observation and listening posts along the fence line. Unfortunately, Cuban soldiers had a little trick up their sleeves that caused a lot of havoc. They would infiltrate our lines (we did repel a lot them, however), find the wire lines that we had laid to the observation and listening posts, cut the wire, and then insert pins through the cut portion on the side that went to the outposts.

These pins were intended to tear open the hands of the Marines who traced the wires in order to find the malfunction, and that is exactly what happened to me. I was working my way through the jungle with the wire in the web of my hand, and searching for the likely cut portion, when I hit one of the sabotaged portions, and cut the hell out of my hand. I wrapped the hand in something, then continued with the wire in the web of my other hand, and shortly tore up that one as well (I was a slow learner!) After that, we put rags around the wire to protect our hands, and ultimately got thick leather gloves, which really did the trick. The scars in the webs of my hands have gotten smaller over the years, but are still visible.

Willie Pete and the Coke Break

The nature of military conflict has changed over the decades, and Coca-Cola has become among the necessary supply items that must be provided! After having strung a spool of wire from a command post to a listening post, I took a "Coke break." The Marine who was manning the post was a pal of mine and had several Cokes in a container. While we should have been inside the observation post, which was a hole dug into the side of a hill and covered with sandbags, we instead were languishing outside, on the roof, shooting the bull and drinking our Cokes.

 Our pleasant evening was interrupted by the firing, in our direction, of a flare gun by a Cuban soldier, which splattered white phosphorus (known as "willie pete") down onto and all over the bunker. The other Marine got the worst of it, and was hit on the neck and part of his face beneath an ear. I got a chuck of it on the fleshy part of my right elbow. It was *very* painful and burned like hell. ("Willie Pete" burns and burns like a 4th-of-July sparkler on steroids until it burns itself out; it cannot even be extinguished with water). A corpsman later treated both of us, but there is not much you can do other than keep clean and as protected as possible. It took months for my elbow to finally heal, and my diminishing scar now just looks like a dirty elbow!

"My Scorpion is Bigger than Yours!"

A field Marine cannot survive unless he overcomes the natural fear that most of us have for bugs, reptiles, spiders, and the like. You certainly don't have to like them, but you need to have some tolerance and not go crazy when they are encountered, including when they crawl on you. It goes with the territory. In Cuba, and the many other "garden spots" that I have visited, you absolutely had to shake the critters out of your boots and clothes before putting them on. We used to have good-natured contests in the morning to see whose boots yielded the largest scorpion!

Thanksgiving Dinner – Turkey and Gnats!

Except for occasional forays into the main part of the base to get a hamburger or hot dog, the three meals we ate daily were "C-Rations." Every now and then was OK, but every day for weeks on end got pretty rough; I got to the point where I was ready to eat cardboard and gargle warm spit as an alternative! We all looked forward to the "hot meal" that was promised for Thanksgiving. Unfortunately, there was a problem; the millions of gnats that wanted to share the meal with us!

The turkey and all the trimmings were brought out into the jungle in vat cans, and all the Marines lined up with our metal mess kits. The gnats were everywhere and there was nothing that could be done to get rid of them. They were on the food in the vat cans, and immediately covered the chow the instant in was dished into in our mess kits. The food appeared black, but it was from the thousands of bugs on top of that food. We had two choices, walk away hungry or eat the bugs as part of the food. Once you got over the psychological hurdles of eating bugs, it wasn't so bad; if fact, you couldn't even taste them. It would have been nice to have also received toothpicks to gets the gnats out of our teeth.

The "Exhibition" and Whorehouse in Panama City

Once the Cuban Missile was over, my battalion was sent back to Camp Pendleton on several World War II era troop ships. I was on the *USS Bexar* APA237 and, all things considered, it was not a bad journey - after all, we were all going to be home for Christmas! We transited the Panama Canal, which was quite an interesting experience that took about eight hours, and then tied up on the Rodman side of the Canal for a day and evening of liberty in Panama City.

A few of my buddies and myself had been told of a "must see" location known as "The Exhibition," where bizarre sexual behavior was rampant, so off we went to find this mysterious place. The information was accurate; it was truly bizarre! It was a giant two-story barn-type of structure with catwalks around both floors, which afforded the visitor an opportunity to see unspeakable debauchery. Every one of the twenty or so stalls, which the observer could lean into for closer looks, had a woman doing something else with an item, person, or animal! I was more scared than fascinated, because I thought we should not be there and might be arrested by the military police. Sure enough, not long after our arrival, a military police car came charging up the dirt road and I just knew we were in big trouble; wrong, the military police officers just joined the tour around the catwalk!

My little group then decided to visit a whorehouse, as a couple of the fellows sought some intimate feminine companionship. After a truly memorable cab ride that I was mistakenly convinced would end in a fiery crash, we ended up at a cathouse. The structure was a very large room with beds lining all the walls, each bed surrounded by a white hospital-like curtain that could be closed for some minor degree of privacy; a woman was seated on each bed. The two horny Marines walked around the room, each picked a woman, paid the roving proprietor, went to the respective bed, pulled the curtain shut, and did whatever they did! I doubt that I have ever been considered a prude, but this pay-as-you-go affection, with some pretty shady ladies in a most unwholesome environment, just was not for me. I managed to "recon the perimeter" until my buddies were finished, and then we all went back to Central Panama City and got drunk.

In many instances, and I suspect that this was one of those instances, I continually reflected on my high school classmates back home, and what they were doing in comparison to what I was doing. They were still in the first semester of their senior year in high school, still picking their zits and whacking off behind the soda shop, and I had just completed my first combat tour of duty as a United States Marine! Very cool!

Smelly Peas on the High Seas

My battalion returned from Cuba on the *USS Bexar* APA237, a WWII Attack Troop Ship. Pulling out of the Panama Canal Zone, my life of leisure doing nothing on the ship ran out and I was assigned to mess duty for the remainder of the voyage back to the United States.

Fortunately, I have never experienced seasickness, but thought that it might have happened then; I never puked, but the very rough seas and greasy spaghetti caused me to come close. One afternoon I was working in the ship's galley with a person who had well-deserved reputation as a shitbird when he took off one boot and sock and actually stirred a giant vat of peas with his dirty and very smelly foot! The ability to take showers (30 seconds under a salt-water faucet after waiting several hours) was pretty much non-existent, and we were all really ripe, and Kurth's actions (pseudonym) were beyond sickening. Since the chow was horrible anyway and Navy cooks (who didn't care about the Marines) were in charge, reporting his actions never occurred to me. In fact, his sweat and toe jam may have added some much needed flavor to that particular vat of peas! Needless to say, I skipped the peas at chow that evening.

Chapter Nine
BACK TO CAMP PENDLETON

My Battalion Lands at White Beach – On Cargo Nets

The Cuban Missile Crisis struck me as a pretty big deal, and I expected a welcome home that would involve bands, speeches, and scores of accolades. That was not to be and, in hindsight, was not very practical because of the hundreds of thousands of American service personnel that played a role. Unlike my outfit, which consisted of very few actually on the island and in contact with Cuban military forces, most other units were afloat offshore in support roles. The big welcome home that some of us expected never materialized. Our ship dropped anchor off the coast of Camp Pendleton; we climbed down nets over the side, and went ashore in assault landing crafts (LCVPs). I did make it home for Christmas and the holidays were pleasant.

My Car had been Trashed at Camp Pendleton!

When the word came down for my unit to "mount out" for what became the Cuban Missile Crisis, the entire base went into lockdown and contact with the outside world ceased. All Marines with personal vehicles had to surrender their keys and vehicles to military policemen for storage during deployment. While I was in Cuba my dad went to the base to retrieve my car, but it would not start. Also, my car was full of stuff that somebody had obviously scrounged from empty offices and storerooms, including a bunch of blank discharge certificates. Someone had obviously used the car while I was deployed, and that someone failed to keep water in the radiator, resulting in the engine seizing up. My dad arranged to have the car towed home and helped pay for the repairs.

David Bushey Passes Away

I got early liberty on Friday, January 18, 1963, and drove home. While I was in Cuba, my parents moved from 1956 Cinco Robles Drive to 1636 Cotter Avenue, both in Duarte and very close to one another. When I got home, my pop asked me to take him to the El Monte Bus Station, because he needed to go to downtown Los Angeles. I drove him to the bus station, dropped him off, and that was the last time I saw him alive.

What I didn't know was that he had been particularly despondent over his deteriorating physical condition, and that my mother sensed that he was potentially on the verge of suicide. He had been ill for many years. His throat cancer had been treated unsuccessfully with radiation, then radical surgery. He then contracted tuberculosis due to weakened resistance, and also had emphysema. Because of his refusal to consent to an additional surgery on his throat, (he just did not feel he could tolerate any more), the City of Hope released him as a patient and that meant the end of legitimate pain medication; (this is as I understood the situation at the time). As a result, he made regular trips to downtown Los Angeles and bought narcotics in the form of seconals from street peddlers, to deal with his pain. He ate very little because everything had a metallic taste, and subsisted primarily on broth. Finally, he was in bed almost all the time. He was a very sick man and I completely understand his frustrations and desire to end his life.

When my mom came home from work she inquired about the whereabouts of my pop, and became very quiet when I told her that he had gone downtown. She did not share her concerns with me, but was fearful that he left to take his life. She was right. The following morning a Sheriff's unit came to our home, and my mom immediately became hysterical; she knew what he had come to tell us. My pop had gone to Los Angeles, bought a bunch of pills, took a bus back to Duarte, bought a quart of beer, checked into a motel on Huntington Drive, and washed the pills down with the beer. The motel was built around a giant oak tree; the motel is long gone, but the oak tree is still there. I think about my pop every time I drive past the oak tree, now surrounded by condominiums, just east of Highland Avenue on the south side of Huntington Drive.

I called my unit and was given emergency leave, and pop was laid to rest at Rose Hills several days later.

The Grand Daddy of Chicken Shit Traffic Citations

A couple of hours after the death notification, I decided to drive over to the Temple City Sheriff's Station to hopefully get a copy of the death report, and learn the details of my pop's death. While southbound on Buena Vista Avenue approaching Duarte Road, I apparently rolled through a stop sign, and was pulled over by a deputy sheriff. He asked for identification and I gave him both my driver's license and my military identification card. He recognized the name and asked if I was related to the man who had taken his own life up on Huntington Drive; he had been at the scene. I replied that the deceased was my dad and that I was en-route to the Temple Station in order to get a copy of the report. He said I should talk to the watch commander. The bastard then issued me a citation for the stop sign!

I then drove to the Temple Station and had a brief meeting with a very nice sergeant, who was the watch commander. The sergeant inquired as to why I came to see him and I told him it was suggested by the deputy who had just given me a ticket. About that time, the deputy who had cited me walked into the station. The sergeant told him to hang on for a minute, then turned to me, extended his condolences and said the report would not be ready for several days. He then indicated for the deputy to follow him out of the lobby area. His body language told me he was surprised over the ticket; he should have canceled it. I was not happy to get the ticket, but it was not until later that I learned just how terribly inappropriate the issuance really was.

An Unexpected Act of Kindness by the First Sergeant

I returned to my unit at Camp Pendleton on the day after my pop's services. I went to the company officer to sign in and close out my leave. I had been given telephonic approval for the leave, which is the military equivalent of vacation time, and needed to complete the processing. The first sergeant was somehow involved in the processing and obviously knew about my situation. That wonderful man tore up the leave papers, which meant that I did not have to use up my leave time for the absence. I don't even recall him saying anything, but he probably muttered a condolence.

The Marine Corps is a unique place. While acknowledging that it has its share of jerks, it also yields some of the most wonderful people on the face of the earth. This simple act of compassion, with few or no words exchanged, absolutely no fanfare, and consummated in about a minute, was among the things that set the standard for my subsequent leadership as a non-commissioned officer and, later, as a commissioned officer. This first sergeant was a decorated WWII veteran, like most of the top enlisted leadership during my first enlistment, and has most likely made his transition to eternal life. I hope things are going well for him up there, and that he has satisfaction for the positive impact that his actions had on lives such as mine.

Drunken Marine Goes Crazy in the Comm' Center

The Communications Platoon had the usual cast of unique characters, and one of them was a big bully from the coal mines of Pennsylvania, "Rat" Ratajac (pseudonym). He was dumb and mean, and even dumber and meaner when he had been drinking. Like most jerks, he did stupid things, and the folks who dealt with his behavior were his superiors. He did not care for them, especially the two staff sergeants whose desks were in the Communications Center.

Late one night, when I was on duty, "Rat" stormed into the comm' center in a drunken rage; my pleas for him to leave were met with a threat to kick my ass. He then approached the desk of one of the two sergeants, opened the middle drawer, and urinated in it! He then went to the desk of the other sergeant, which had a carousel of smoking pipes on top of it, and commenced to subject each pipe stem to some indignities that I will leave to the imagination! He then stumbled out and went back to the barracks.

Holy shit, now what do I do? Reporting him was not much of an option, and would have been hazardous to my health. I spent the rest of the night trying to undo his damage. I carefully drained and cleaned out the drawer; it wasn't easy or pleasant. I still remember drying the upside drawer over the heater and carefully cleansing all the inside items. I threw a few things away, liked urine soaked papers, and was hoping they would not be missed. I cleaned the pipes as best I could, but certainly would not have wanted to smoke one!

I was successful in covering up this foolish and gross incident. I thought that "Rat" would brag about the things he did to the two sergeants, but never heard a word, or even a visual acknowledgement when he and I interacted. I came to believe that the dumb bastard did not even recall the incident. I sure did, though, and wish that I didn't! This was one of those times when I asked myself if I should have stayed in high school, as it would have been my junior year. I did learn a lesson from this incident; if you smoke pipes, never leave them where they are accessible to someone who may not care for you!

Pay Call – Primitive By Today's Standards

Today, a young man or woman in the military is paid reasonably well, and the pay is deposited directly into the service member's personal bank account. This has not always been the case. For the first few years that I was in the Corps, we were paid in cash every two weeks, typically mid-week as I recall, by a junior commissioned officer. We would stand in the pay line, approach a table behind which was seated a lieutenant who was always armed with a .45 on his duty belt, with a disbursing clerk seated to the side. We would approach; stand at attention, and then sound off with our name and serial number. The disbursing clerk would say something to the effect, "sir, this Marine is due twenty-one dollars and seventy-three cents." The lieutenant would remove the stated amount from the money tray in front of him, and count it out for the Marine standing there. The Marine would indicate, "thank you sir," step back a pace, do an about face, and depart. The same process would be repeated for every man in the unit.

The amount of money described above seems pretty low by today's standards, but that is just about the amount that I received each two weeks during my overseas assignments. As a private first class, my monthly pay was $81.00. After taxes and the allotment (savings) that I had taken out, those paydays were pretty lean.

"Five for Seven" – Financial Wizards

Most units had a financial wizard who successfully preyed on fiscally irresponsible kids like me. I *always* ran out of money two or three days before payday, and believe that I was pretty typical of the other young kids in my unit. These wizards would loan kids like me $5.00, but with the understanding that they would be repaid $7.00 a couple of days later. I wish that I had been able to save enough money to have been one of these businessmen! I suspect that this business acumen had persevered and that most of these folks are now venture capitalists or pawn shop owners.

Captain A. J. Squared-Away – Not!

While his last name escapes me, in my platoon we had a total shitbird whose first and middle names started with the letters A and J, and like everyone else with those initials, he was referred to as "AJ." He was incompetent and arrogant, and those were his good qualities. We used to marvel at how "AJ" even got through boot camp. After a year or so in the Corps, he was still a buck private, and that was hard to do! Since he was the antithesis of being squared away, we kiddingly referred to him as "Private A. J. Squared Away."

One Monday morning, a sergeant from the base brig, (military jail), showed up to clean out AJ's locker. It seems that AJ was walking around San Clemente wearing captain's bars on his collar. In addition to violating every sacred rule in the Marine Corps, this idiot pulled his little stunt in the community where all of us routinely went on liberty, and it was a virtual certainty that several people recognized whom he really was. Over and above facial recognition, Marine captains have a demeanor that AJ could never replicate. I occasionally think of ole' AJ and wonder what became of him; it was not likely to be anything good.

Hitchhiking to and from Camp Pendleton

It is rare to see folks hitchhiking these days, but that was not always the case. During my service as an enlisted Marine, hitchhiking was very common, especially among servicemen. I was fortunate in having a car after boot camp and had that car, a 1952 Ford Victoria, up until just a couple of months before deploying to the Orient. In preparation for deployment, I sold it to another Marine for a reasonable price, but that left me without a set of wheels for my last few weeks in the States. During this time, I pretty much hitchhiked to and from the base to my home on the weekends, and never had any problems to speak of; people were almost always good to men in uniform. When returning to the base on Sunday afternoons, my mom or pop would typically drive me to a major street from which I could start hitchhiking back to Camp Pendleton. The one area of concern and caution was around Laguna Beach, because of the many homosexual men who tried to convince hitchhiking servicemen to take a diversion for inappropriate activities; I was hit on a couple of times, but it was always polite and subtle and did not get at all nasty when I made it clear that I was not interested. I appreciated the rides!

My Senior Prom

Had I not dropped out of high school, I *might* have graduated in June of 1963 with the rest of my classmates. They did graduate and I was invited to attend what would have been my senior prom. This was a very satisfying event for me. I showed up in my dress uniform, a pretty girl on my arm, a medal on my chest (sharpshooter), a stripe on my sleeve, and a very confident demeanor. Plus, I got my GED over a year before! All of the guys were sweating the draft, which affected just about all-eligible males in those days, but I had half of my military service behind me. As a person who had previously been seen as the most likely to fail, this was a very satisfying event for me.

"Lock-On" Training and Deployment to the Orient

During the late 1950s and into the mid 1960s, the Marine Corps had a concept known as "transplacement" battalions. The West Coast Battalions, following approximately 18 months in the United States, rotated to the 3rd Marine Division in the Orient for a 13-month tour of duty. During the stateside portion of the rotation, the old timers transfer out and the new folks transfer in. As the battalions passed each other in the Pacific, they exchange designations and took on the identity of the other. My Battalion, 2nd Battalion, 1st Marine Regiment, 1st Marine Division, became the 3rd Battalion, 9th Marine Regiment, 3rd Marine Division. We were then known as "3/9."

However, before this rotation, the Battalion went through an extensive six-week orientation package, known as "Lock On" training. It was very heavy in combat and field activities, and intended to sharpen the battalion's ability to immediately deploy into a combat situation. All leaves had already been taken, but as someone who lived in Southern California, I still managed to get home for most weekends until we actually shipped out.

Note: *All of the aforementioned Marine Corps activities occurred during what would have been my junior and senior high school years, had I not dropped out and entered the military on my 17th birthday.*

Chapter Ten
THE ORIENT – THIRD BATTALION, NINTH MARINE REGIMENT (3/9)

In July of 1963, after having served a very eventful year and a half or so in Battalion 2/1, I became a member of the 3rd Battalion of the 9th Marine Regiment, of the 3rd Marine Division. My entire previous battalion (2/1) shipped overseas and was re-designated as 3/9, with that unit returning to the United States and being re-designated as one of the battalions of the 1st Marine Division at Camp Pendleton. Although the base of operations for 3/9 was at Camp Hanson on the island of Okinawa, where the division headquarters was located, all of the battalions of the 3rd Division deployed frequently around the Orient.

Setting Sail for the Orient

The battalion departed San Diego for the Orient on the *USS Patrick*, a large dependent and troop ship, one of several that moved constantly to and from the Orient, moving troops and dependents. We departed from the exact pier where mom, pop, and I watched my brother, Larry, depart for Korea some ten years earlier. I insisted that mom and Larry not come to San Diego to watch the ship leave; instead we said our goodbyes in Duarte during my last liberty. I still recalled the emotions of watching my brother's ship, the *USS Mann*, the same type of vessel, depart San Diego Bay and disappear into the evening sunset, and did not want me or my family to go through that again. The voyage took about two weeks, and included one-day stops in Hawaii and Guam.

Coke and the Half Order of Coleslaw

The ship pulled into Pearl Harbor, and we all got a nice look at the then-new Arizona War Memorial, which had just been completed. Payday was still several days away, and I was just about broke. I hitchhiked to Waikiki Beach, and went to the sands by the military facility, Fort Derussy, which at that time was nothing more than a hut where you could buy refreshments and borrow floaters and bathing suits. I borrowed a bathing suit, swam for a while, and then blew my entire wad of seventy-five cents on a Coke and a half order of coleslaw. I was told there was a dance that evening at the USO in Downtown Honolulu; sounded good so I walked over there.

While in Hawaii I took a bunch of photos. One of the rolls of film was in color, which in those days was incredibly expensive (at least on my pay!) to develop, and I ultimately threw the roll away. How stupid, in hindsight!

"Servicemen Welcome, No Uniforms Allowed"

I got to the USO (United Service Organization) early, as it was still daylight, but that was not the problem. On the marquee in front of the building, the letters read (this is exact; I will never forget what it said): "DANCE TONIGHT, SERVICEMEN WELCOME, NO UNIFORMS ALLOWED." I was in my tropical uniform ("trops") and had no other clothes, as in those day it was prohibited for servicemen to have civilian clothes on a naval vessel. I was out of luck, and hitchhiked back to ship. This situation really irritated me, and left a bad taste in my mouth for the USO for a number of years, but I came to realize that this poor practice, obviously intended to keep the number of service personnel attending the dance at a manageable level, was the rare exception, and that the USO is a great organization.

This prohibition of civilian clothes on naval vessels is why every port had "locker clubs,' where the sailors, and seagoing Marines, could keep civilian clothes. It was the norm for personnel to have a locker with "civvies" in every port they regularly visited. These clubs usually included lounges, tailor shops, and gift shops. They were almost always in a part of town that also had a fair share of tattoo parlors and burlesque shows.

Unique Barometric Pressure and the "Jewelry Box" Smell

We arrived at Naha Harbor, Okinawa, late in the afternoon, and were bussed almost to the other end of the Island, to Camp Hansen, which was named for a World War II Medal of Honor recipient from the Battle of Okinawa. I still remember my fascination with the atmospheric conditions, with pretty skies, rapid high moving clouds, and a most pleasant pressure in the air. I still remember that the inside of our open barracks had the same odor as the Japanese jewelry boxes that I had seen in my life, including a couple that my brother had sent to our mother years earlier. Funny the things you remember. Each structure was two cement barracks, each capable of housing about sixty Marines, joined by a common head (bathroom) in the center.

During the day, a number of Okinawan nationals spent time in the barracks spit-shining our shoes and laundering our clothes. As I recall, I paid $5 a payday for complete maintenance of all my uniforms, and daily spit shining of my shoes and boots. We did not make much money, but this was still a great deal.

Navy Ships of my Enlisted Era – World War II Vintage

Without exception, every amphibious troop ship that I served on in the 1960s was a veteran of World War II. They had all seen a great deal of combat at the landings of Guadalcanal, Tarawa, Iwo Jima, Saipan, Guam, Okinawa, etc. For our amphibious exercises we crawled over the same sides and rode in the same small landing crafts that carried some many brave men ashore, and returned so many of their remains back to the ships. Some of the ships were the *USS Bayfield* APA33, *USS Bexar* APA237, *USS Henrico* APA45, *USS Clymer* APA27, *USS Union* AKA106, *USS Princeton* LPH5, and the *USS Cabildo* LSD16. Boy, if only those ships could talk. None of these exist anymore, as the last few decades have seen a tremendous building program for the "Gator Navy."

Interesting note: While in the final stages of writing this book, I found myself teaching a leadership course at the Henrico County Police Department in Virginia. The U.S.S. Henrico was built and launched during World War II, and named after this county. I had a nice chat with a few Virginians who had a sense of history, and who enjoyed hearing about my experiences on this ship.

War Debris Littered the Harbor in Guam

The ship made a brief visit to Guam between Hawaii and Okinawa. As we entered the harbor, there were still scores of beached landing crafts, all rusty and battered, left over from the American landing at Guam in 1944. I was struck by the stifling nature of the temperature and humidity, and had a new appreciation for the American forces which made the landing and fought on Guam in World War II, as the campaign was at almost the identical time of the year as my brief visit. I spent my few hours of liberty walking around the abandoned Japanese airfield adjacent to the built-up base areas, just reflecting on the historic nature of the Island. At this time, there were still at least two Japanese soldiers, left over from World War II who were living in the jungle, and refused to believe the war was over!

Women in the Men's Head

On my first day at Camp Hansen, I was in the head, sitting on the pot, doing what I do best, when an Okinawan woman walked in and sat right next to me! Marine Corps heads are typically not places for people who like privacy, and this one had a long row of toilets with no dividers, but having a female share the facilities was a new experience for me. I was horrified, tried to look away, and got out of there as fast as I could. By the end of my first tour in the Orient, these types of encounters usually resulted in casual conversations. The Marine Corps is not a place for people who cannot overcome inhibitions, and those who join the Corps with inhibitions usually leave without them.

The Great Fudge Disaster

After a few months overseas, I got a real hankering for chocolate fudge, so wrote home and asked my mom to whip up a batch, wrap it good, and send it to me. Now this was not a quick turnaround, as *all* mail went by ship, so it took at least three weeks for a letter to get home, and another three weeks to get a response; the box of fudge arrived about six weeks after I asked her to send it. On the day it arrived, we were all gathered around for mail call, and I opened the box the minute it was given to me. Big mistake! Within seconds, all the fudge was gone, snatched-up by the numerous hands that reached into the box! I was devastated. I wrote another letter home, telling mom what had occurred, and asked her to send another box. When the next box arrived, about another six weeks later, I took the package without saying anything to anyone. I stashed the box in my wall locker and never took a piece out unless I was sure that no one was looking! I think the box lasted me for two or three days.

Burning Butts on the High Seas

This was really funny. We were on a troop ship; I think it was the *USS Henrico* APA45, going someplace that I don't recall. The head, like the head on most troop ships, had a long trough, with a series of wooden slats to sit on, as the toilet for bowel movements. Seawater moved constantly from one end of the trough to the other, washing away the human waste. One day someone devised an incendiary device that looked something like a hot dog container, but more sturdy, with higher sides, and filled it with wadded-up issue paper. This unknown person ignited his creation, set it adrift at one end of the trough, and ran like hell, disappearing into the annals of history.

As the device made its way in the current down the trough it passed under each Marine seated, all of whom had their pants down to their ankles, and burned their butts! The yelling and screaming and profanities could be heard for some distance. This was horrible, just horrible; I wish that I had thought of it! The suspect absolutely would have been beaten within an inch of his life had his identity been discovered.

My Second (And Last!) Industrial Grade Hangover

The horrible hangover that I experienced at Camp San Mateo a year or two prior should have taught me a lesson and it did, but not enough of a lesson. A few of us spent a night of bar hopping in Kin Village, just outside the Camp Hansen Gate on Okinawa. As I recall, I was cautious not to drink different types of alcohol, and also not to eat exotic food while drinking, but I sure as hell did something wrong. I still recall the spectacle I created for the officer-of-the-day and the sergeant-of-the-guard as I vomited in pain on the back steps of the barracks. In my younger days, there was some type of a restriction in my esophagus that made vomiting very painful, and literally took me to my knees, and that is what was occurring. Although almost fifty years ago, I can still see those two fellows watching my painful performance, and shaking their heads in amusement.

Horrible Racism on Okinawa

I witnessed and experienced much worse racism in the military than in civilian life, and it was at its worse in Okinawa. While Marines of all ethnicities seemed to get along OK while on duty and on the base, off-duty and off the base was a much different story. The dividing lines between the bars that catered to whites and blacks might just as well have been painted on the ground; they were that discernible. Hispanics were considered to be white. While there were a few bars that were somewhat transient and open to all, most of the bars were territorial with respect to units and race. While a black walking into a white bar might have been unpleasant, a white walking into a black bar may well have been fatal.

While I was on the island, a white military police officer had to literally shoot his way out of a military police sub-station in a place called "the Four Corners," which was part of the city of Koza. I recall a black Marine who was in my platoon and with whom I thought I had a good relationship, but I was mistaken; the hostility he exhibited to me and some of my pals when we encountered he and a group of his pals out in Kin Village was really ugly. At times the situation was so bad that Marines had to wear the tropical uniform with a tie when out in the village, the theory being that Marines were less likely to fight if it meant messing up the uniform; plus, anyone who returned to the base with a messed-up uniform could be easily recognized as a combatant. During particularly difficult times, there were actually Marine observers with radios on key rooftops so as to be able to report problems to the roving staff non-commissioned officer "courtesy patrols" which frequented the village.

Violent Death Behind the Command Post

One morning a group of shirtless men descended on my battalion. These were military police criminal investigators who had removed their utility jackets so the folks they were interviewing were not aware of their rank; (some of the investigators were likely to be of lesser rank than some of the people they would be interviewing, and military protocol was for rank to not to be a factor in criminal interviews). It seemed that a murder victim had been found in the reservoir behind the battalion command post, and an obvious attempt was underway to investigate the circumstances. I do recall that it was clearly believed to have been racially motivated, but I do not recall the ethnicity of the victim, and never learned any of the details or whether it was ever solved. My perception was that the black racists were the more likely to commit acts of violence, but that there were a few "good ol' boys" from the south who would not have given a second thought to following in the white racist footsteps of some of their KKK kinfolk. Camp Hansen could be a pretty dangerous place at times.

Despicable Behavior by a Small Number of Jerks

The vast majority of the Marines that I served with were decent and honorable men, who treated the Okinawan people with dignity, respect, and goodwill. Unfortunately, there were a few real jerks, and their foolish behavior could be at all-time highs when encountering burial tombs while on field exercises. It was common in the case of deaths of Okinawans to place *sake*, an alcoholic drink, in the tombs with the deceased. Occasionally, some idiot Marine would break into the tombs, then take and drink the *sake*. This conduct was absolutely despicable and added validity to the island's detractors who criticized the American military presence there.

Death Of President Kennedy

November 22, 1963, for a tragic day for all Americans, and for the world. This was the day President John F. Kennedy was assassinated in Dallas by that despicable little weasel, Lee Harvey Oswald. I learned of the president's death when I fell in for formation, in the battalion's open area, at about 0530. Unlike the highly emotional scenes in the United States, I saw no crying or breakdowns, but the following days were sad and solemn. All military forces went on "high alert" just in case it was an act orchestrated by a foreign power; however the forces stood down after several days.

This was a bad time for me for another reason. I had been officially invited to the christening of the *USS J. C. England*, DLG-22, named after the son of my godparents, Sam and Thelma England, who perished on the battleship *Oklahoma* during the December 7, 1941, Japanese attack on Pearl Harbor. I thought there was a chance, and there may have been, that I could have been given TAD orders (Temporary Additional Duty orders) for Long Beach to attend as official guest; I will never know whether I had a chance, because the 30-day period of mourning put a damper on everything, including the christening which became a quick and quiet affair.

Postscript: In early 1991, on temporary orders to mainland Japan with a stopover in Okinawa, I went back to Camp Hansen. Standing on the exact spot where I had been standing when informed of President Kennedy's death, just outside the battalion headquarters, was among the several places I visited that day on the nostalgic walk back down "memory lane."

My Burning Butt in the Hot Box in Koza

As a young Marine on the island of Okinawa, I decided to get one of those massages that I heard had heard so much about. I went to the city of Koza and found a massage parlor, and the price for the complete massage and accompanying services (not sexual!) was $1.82. The first thing that I was instructed to do was disrobe and get into a steam box, after which I would be washed from head to toe by a pretty girl, and then given a massage. There was a glitch however, that came to light when the gal locked me into the hot box and then apparently forgot about me! After about 15 minutes I was really in misery, and my rear end was on these hot wooden planks and burning like hell. I did the best I could to get my rear end off the planks inside the box by putting my neck up against the back of the box for support, but I was in real misery until the gal finally came back and let me out of that damn box. I went back a few more times but made the girl remain nearby when I was in the hot box.

While I never availed myself of the "additional services," some of the gals provided an array of sexual services in addition to the massages. I was saving myself, but in hindsight I am not sure what I was saving myself for!

Very Kind and Considerate Japanese People

I will never forget, nor will I cease to be grateful, for the very nice and helpful way that the Japanese and Okinawans treated me when I was a young Marine. At the time, it seemed like World War II had been in the distant past, but as I look back and reflect on how time really flies by, I realized not such a long time had passed since "the great war to end all wars" - only a mere eighteen years. In both countries (Okinawa was not part of Japan at that time, but the two were later reunited into one country – Japan), some traumatic remnants of the war were still in evidence, such as pockmarked structures.

I still recall one particular act of kindness; when at Camp Fuji on mainland Japan, I was at a train station in Gotemba and clearly experiencing consternation at trying to figure out how to get to Yukosuka. A bi-lingual Japanese man recognized my plight, and found a man who was going to the first of several towns where I would need to switch trains, he handed me off to that man, who handed me off to another at another station, and so on until I reached Yokosuka – and none, other than the first man, spoke English. I never forgot this, and other acts of kindness, and always sought to be just as helpful and gracious to Japanese persons visiting Los Angeles.

I returned to both Okinawa and Mainland Japan in 1992. While just about all whom I encountered on the street were cordial, the previous widespread exceptional warmth was gone.

Prostitution in the Orient

During my entire time in the Marine Corps, there was always an abundance of prostitutes wherever Marines could be found. While in the 3rd Marine Division, the greatest concentrations were on Okinawa and in the Philippines. In reflecting on that era, I don't recall blatant prostitution in mainland Japan, but am certain that it existed also. My time in Korea was out in the boondocks in the middle of a freezing winter, but I am sure even then prostitutes could be found. Prostitution was not encouraged or discouraged, nor seen as bad or good; it was just an absolute reality of overseas military life. It was just as common for a Marine to say he was going to "get laid" as it was to be going to a movie or to get a meal in town.

The "going rate" for the services of a prostitute during that era was $2 for a "short time" and $5 for an "over-nighter." These "flat rates" were pretty much standard throughout all of the counties in the Pacific that I visited. My battalion never got to Australia, and I suspect that prostitution would have been very limited in that country.

I was among the very few Marines who actually got some degree of lecturing on prostitutes, because of my occasional duties as a cryptographer, access to classified materials, and my security clearance. There were instances where female spies, acting on behalf of the Soviet Union, would compromise American servicemen with sexual escapades, and then blackmail them to gain classified information. This was a real problem for service personnel in Europe, especially Germany, but realistically not so much for a low-level person such as myself in an infantry battalion where our classified material was relatively low level.

As I have said previously, I never availed myself of the services of a prostitute. I cannot say that my abstinence was based on morality; I was just never interested in assembly-line affection.

My Girlfriend from Saipan

I was much less amorous than most of my fellow Marines on Okinawa, but I did fall briefly under the romantic spell of a pretty little gal from Saipan, whose name was Heidico. She worked in a bar (every pretty girl on Okinawa worked in a bar!), and most likely was not actually as angelic as she appeared to be. Nevertheless, we got together on several occasions and genuinely enjoyed each other's company. I honestly do not recall how our relationship ended, probably just drifted in different directions. The relationship was casual and not committed, and to this day I occasionally wonder what happened to her. In the background of the relationship was the *very strong and continuous admonition* of my Mom to not marry and bring an Asian bride back home; she was afraid that such a union could yield grandchildren that might be taken back to the Orient if the marriage failed.

Venereal Disease Worked to my Advantage

Military regulations are such that self-reporting of venereal disease is encouraged so that immediate and appropriate medical attention can be provided, and a Marine cannot be disciplined as long as he immediately reports his condition. Our company commander decided, however, that he would not promote anyone who had VD, and this worked out great for me. In late 1963, 57 percent of the men in H&S Company reportedly were being treated for VD, and a number of these folks were senior to me and likely to be promoted ahead of me – except for their delicate conditions. I ended up being promoted sooner than would otherwise have occurred because of all the amorous Marines in my outfit! Part of my military success is attributed to VD!

I Finally Made Lance Corporal

When I made PFC out of boot camp, I just knew that I would make lance corporal in record time as well; I was wrong! I got to add the crossed rifles under my single stripe, the insignia of lance corporal, in November of 1963. At the time, we were undergoing cold weather training at Camp Fuji, which was on the island of Hokkaido, beneath the famous long-dormant volcano. It was to be another sixteen or so months before I was promoted again. Although I was in an infantry battalion where promotions were pretty good, I was not classified as an infantryman, but rather a communicator, and the fastest rank generally went to those Marines in the infantry companies as opposed to the Headquarters & Service Company where I was assigned. It was a thrill to write home and put that coveted "LCpl" on my return address, and I can still recall the first time I answered the phone in the Communications Center with my new rank.

"Blood Stripes" and Disabled Arms

For decades there was a unique Marine Corps tradition of "pinning the stripes" on newly promoted Marines. The newly promoted man would walk through a column of other Marines, (of either the same or higher rank of the new promotee), and each of the folks on either side of the column would slug the new promotee in the arm where the stripes would go. At the end of the column, the new promotee would turn around and walk back through the column so that everyone had the opportunity to "pin the stripes" on both of the new promotee's arms.

Let there be no doubt, these were not polite taps on the arm, but in most cases slugs as hard as the senior men could hit! When I made lance corporal, there were about 20 or 30 folks in the two columns, and each one hit me twice. After this promotion ritual, the arms of the new promotee were typically black and blue for several days, and pretty much useless for a day or so.

About a year and a half later, when stationed at the Marine Corps Air Station at El Toro (since deactivated and torn down), I went through the same ritual when I made corporal, but the column of "well-wishers) was slightly smaller because there were fewer people of my rank or above in the communications center where I was assigned. One additional "treat" that I did not experience was the tradition in some units of also "pinning the blood stripe" (the red stripe on the trouser legs of the dress blue uniform for non-commissioned officers) where the same two columns were used to slug each newly promoted non-commissioned officer on the upper leg between the waist and the knees. In those ceremonies it was not unusual for the new promotee to actually have trouble walking for a brief period of time. Again, folks did not "pull their punches," but typically struck with all the force they could muster.

Stupid Kids and Classified Materials

Late one night, during a detail to destroy classified materials, I was among a couple of other young Marines who were still acting like high school idiots, except we had some expensive toys to play with. For reasons that I no longer recall, while at Camp Hanson we destroyed our classified materials by incineration at White Beach at night. One evening I and two other young Marines, in a large USMC van, full of classified materials to be destroyed, decided to have some fun by driving the van all over White Beach, including maneuvers pretty close to the waterline. Unfortunately, with a van full of classified materials, we got badly stuck in the muck, and the tide was rising! With an incredible stroke of good luck, I found an Army unit nearby that had a tank retriever (tow truck on steroids!), and the soldier was nice enough to extricate the van from the mess we were in. We quickly performed our destruction duties and got back to the base. I was sweating bullets over this issue, and was certain that I and the other two kids would have been severely disciplined if our foolish behavior had come to light. Doing stupid stuff is bad enough, but doing stupid stuff when in possession of classified materials is pretty serious. This was among the lessons that I learned that contributed to my maturity. Had I not found the soldier with the tank retriever, this could have been a pretty nasty "fork in my road!"

Great Sleep in the Back of a Bouncing Truck

I have just about always had trouble staying awake as a passenger in a vehicle. This has not always been a bad thing, because I have usually been able to sleep like a baby in the back of a bouncing truck when lying on equipment! Reflecting on my military experience in the field, which was pretty extensive, I usually slept just fine as long as I was warm and dry, which was not always easy but which I usually managed to achieve. I mastered the art of staying warm by always creating an outer shell made up of either a poncho or a shelter half (in that era, each Marine in the field carried one half of a tent that was referred to as a shelter, thus a shelter half), and also – circumstances permitting – by removing my outer clothing and boots. The nightmare for me was trying to sleep in a foxhole with several inches of water in the bottom.

Really Cold Showers

I will never forget the cold showers at Camp Fuji! On a daily basis, we bathed out of our helmets using water we heated in large drums. However, before going on liberty on weekends, we really needed a complete shower. If there was ever hot water, it was always gone by the time peons like me got to the showers. It was winter and really cold, and the water came from nearby streams. I will always remember others and me dashing in, screaming profanities, quickly soaping down, and rinsing off. It was not a pleasant experience, but we got most of the big chunks of dirt off.

A Very Kind Gunny at Camp Fuji

While at Camp Fuji, my mom sent me an audiotape, thinking that I had ready access to a tape recorder. It was a reel, and required a recorder that was not easily found. Someone said that the H&S company gunny, Gunnery Sergeant L. Faulkner, had such a device. I went to GySgt. Faulkner, and he could not have been nicer. He did have a recorder, took me in his tent, set it up where all I had to do was hit the start key, and then left so I could be alone as I listened to my mom. What a wonderful and gracious man, and an act of kindness that I never forgot. It was another incident that reflected the type of behavior that I have tried to emulate. Gunny Faulkner will always be one of my heroes.

Almost thirty years later, as a lieutenant colonel and commanding officer of 3rd ANGLICO, I invited a close friend and former Marine, Jack Claven, to be my guest at our Marine Corps birthday ball. He asked if he could bring to the ball his dear friend, a retired Marine and the man who saved his life by carrying him to safety on Iwo Jima. Certainly I said it would be an honor. Cathy and I drove to Jack's house in Glendora to get Jack, his wife Alice, and his friend. It was Retired Gunnery Sergeant Faulkner, who I immediately recognized! What a thrill and a most enjoyable evening. The gunny had retired in Barstow, and spent many years as a volunteer armorer for the Barstow Police Department. He and Jack have both made that transition to eternal life, and I have every confidence that heaven is a better place because of the presence of those wonderful men and Marines.

Snuggled Like a Bug in a Rug at Camp Fuji

In the big scheme of things, I cannot imagine that this issue will be of much value to the reader, but it is one of those things that, for whatever reason, I sometimes think about. Camp Fuji, at the base of the dormant volcano Mount Fuji, was a very cold place between November and January, which is the time period when I was first there. There were no buildings at the upper base camp where my unit was assigned, so we slept in large tents alongside all of our equipment. There was not much to do most evenings except gamble, and as a result most of us "hit the sack" pretty early. I don't think I have ever had better sleep in my life. We were on cots, and used our ponchos and shelter halves to create a seal around the cotton sleeping bags; although down-filled, they were not adequate for the low temperatures, but the seals we created made them very toasty. I still remember snuggling and thinking about all of the things that eighteen year old kids think about, probably like all of the other kids in that tent who were also wedged between weapons and communications equipment.

The Fingerprint Expert

In preparation for deployment to the Orient, I thought I would do something that would help prepare me for a career in law enforcement. I enrolled in an extensive correspondence course, through the Institute of Applied Science in Chicago, on fingerprinting, classifications, and related topics. I spent literally scores of hours on my lessons, and finally completed the course, and got my diploma as a fingerprint classification expert, after returning to the United States. Other than occasionally using my knowledge to determine the primary fingerprint classification of a person whose identity was in question, and comparing it with the files in Records and Identifications Division, this specialized education was never of value to me as a police officer. It was, however, of tremendous value as it kept me busy and out of the bars while overseas!

Focused On A Law Enforcement Career

In 2013, I decided to get serious about trying to reestablish contact with some of the men whom I had served with in the Orient. While I bumped into Larry Schaetzel several years prior, and had a great chat, up until then he was about the only one that I spoke to after our service together. With the magic of the Internet, and my great computer wizard buddy, Ron Caron, I managed to contact Rich Humbert and Hank Stegman from the 3/9, and Dave Leslie and Jim Collier. In our chats, these folks mentioned that it was clear that I was focused on a career in law enforcement. Guess my intentions were more conspicuous than I realized.

Bar Fight in Sasebo

During a port call in Sasebo (Japan), I went barhopping with my good pal, John Kraus. As we were sitting in a bar and enjoying a cold beer, a drunken sailor came up and announced that it was a Navy bar, and ordered us to leave. I humored him, said that we were all Americans, and asked that we be able to finish our beers before leaving; he said OK and staggered off. A few minutes later I heard a thump and saw something fly past my face. The sailor delivered a sucker punch to the side of John's head, and it was his glasses that sailed past me!

John was as blind as a bat without his glasses and dropped to the floor to find them. I took off after the drunk sailor and he ran out what he mistakenly thought was an exit door, but which was an internal door that went inside the back of the bar. He quickly ran back out, but in so doing swung the bamboo door so hard that it was penetrated by the edge of the bar. At this point, three or four Japanese men (who you never saw in bars that catered to Americans) emerged from the back and started to kick the crap out of the sailor! Now the game had changed and Japanese men were beating the American sailor, who was clearly a drunken jerk, but still an American. I jumped into the fray and started pulling the Japanese men off the sailor, who ultimately broke free and fled out the front door. The Japanese men disappeared into the back, John found his glasses, and we went back to our beer.

A few minutes later I heard a commotion outside the bar, then two shore patrolmen, a Marine sergeant and a Navy petty officer, came into the bar. It seems the drunken sailor started rounding up a bunch of other drunken sailors to return to the bar and kick my butt for supposedly kicking his. He had me confused me with the group of Japanese men who had jumped him. The matter was quickly sorted out; the group that the squid (sailor) had assembled to do a number on me was dispersed, we all shook hands, and the matter was over. I remain grateful that the shore patrol intercepted the Navy crowd before it reached me!

The Typewriter Crisis at Camp Hansen

This was truly a crisis for me, and I thought I was going to be in big trouble. On New Year's night, just before ringing in 1964, I had the all- night duty at the Communication Center in Camp Hansen, on Okinawa. Our typewriter was not working, so I went across the hallway and borrowed the special typewriter used by the S-3 Section (Operations & Training). It was a very unique typewriter with a long carriage, and used for typing stencils. I carried it over and placed it on a counter, and was typing letters home while seated on a stool. I leaned back too far and started to fall, but broke my backwards fall by putting a foot up to the counter; my foot caught the typewriter and sent this heavy machine flying across the room! When it landed, it broke into several pieces.

I was horrified beyond description and knew that the S-3 chief, a crusty old and mean gunny sergeant, would really make it hard on me. It was clear that I could not fix the typewriter.

One of the Marines in my platoon however, Richard Garlock, had been a typewriter repairman in civilian life. I could not wait for daylight to drag him over to the battalion headquarters to hopefully fix the typewriter. It was now New Year's Day and Bob was like everyone else and wanted to sleep in, but apparently saw the horror in my eyes and reluctantly accompanied me back to see what he could do with the broken typewriter. He took one look and announced that it was destroyed and even with replacement parts, which he obviously had no access to, it was a goner! I begged him to try to at least reassemble it, to conceal my actions; he agreed and managed to get it so it looked OK, but the carriage would not even move.

The following day was a workday and I was in the building when the S-3 folks came to work. The clerk immediately went to the typewriter, found that it would not work, and complained to the gunny. The gunny said something about it being a worthless piece of crap and told the clerk to have it sent to supply to be replaced. That was it! To say that I was relieved is an understatement.

Screwing Over a Dispersing Clerk – Very Bad Idea

This is one of the very few situations that I did not personally witness, but am aware of, and a story that must not be permitted to be forgotten. Barry Morrison, who I later served with on the Los Angeles Police Department, served in the Marine Corps and his specialty was dispersing. While on a Western Pacific (Westpac) deployment, he developed a very strong dislike for a certain staff sergeant, and decided to make that person's life miserable. The most enjoyable event on Westpac cruises was the much-anticipated visit to the Philippines towards the end of the deployment. For several months before that port call, Barry overpaid the staff sergeant by several dollars on each of the bi-monthly paydays, and timed his treachery to come to a head just before the visit to Subic Bay, when instead of cash (that is how we were paid in those days) the sergeant was informed that he had mistakenly been overpaid, and that he actually owed money to the government! Pissing off a dispersing clerk is not a good idea.

The South China Sea and Forty Below Zero

My battalion was "afloat" and participating in an exercise along the Korean coast in the middle of winter, which included an amphibious landing from the South China Sea. I couldn't believe my good luck, as I was given duty aboard the ship, the *USS Bayfield* APA33 (which was the command ship for the WWII Normandy Landing on Jun 6, 1944!) My job consisted of receiving and decoding classified message traffic, and taking classified material ashore as a courier.

Life aboard a troop ship when all the Marines were aboard was pretty lousy; long lines for everything, mediocre chow, and crowded stuffy quarters. On the other hand, when the troops were ashore, being aboard was the best; the sailors broke out the best food, no lines for anything, and generally a relaxed environment. As someone who was always in the dirt on field exercises, I couldn't believe my good luck on this particular operation!

About the second day of my great duty, a classified message needed to be taken ashore. My job was to make a quick run to and from the beach and back in paradise within an hour or so. Wrong! It was colder than hell, about 40 degrees below, and we all had heavy cold winter gear, but I saw no need to don all this specialized clothing for a quick trip ashore; my landing boat would be met by another classified courier to take my pouch, and then I would quickly return to the ship. All I wore was my field jacket with the nylon liner, which was a big mistake!

I climbed down the cargo net into a "peter boat" (LCVP small landing craft), experienced about a ten-minute trip to the beach, handed over the classified pouch, and was on the way back to the ship; then the problems developed. The seas had picked up and were becoming so rough that the landing craft could not pull up alongside the ship, nor could it return to the beach without the real possibility of breaching (being flung sideways)!

By this time, I was freezing my ass off! After about *four hours* of bobbing around like a cork, the landing craft was able to pull into the well deck of the *USS Cabildo* LSD16 (landing ship dock, where the entire rear of the ship was open to facilitate small craft entering and departing). After starting to thaw out, a very considerate sailor took me to the ship's galley where a cook made the best ham sandwich I have ever eaten, and then pointed out a berthing area with vacant bunks where I crashed for the night. By the next morning, the seas had settled down and I caught a shuttle back to the *USS Bayfield*. Needless to say, I learned a very valuable lesson; when in doubt, wear all your cold weather gear!

Unwanted Butt Buddy on the USS Cabildo

During my brief unintended stay on the *USS Cabildo*, the kind sailor described in the previous paragraph warned me about an unidentified serial sodomist who was loose on the ship, and who on several occasions jumped into a sailor's bunk, in a crowed berthing area, clamped his hand over the victim's mouth, placed a knife to the throat, and committed sodomy. In the berthing area I selected a bunk pretty close to a hatch (door) that was adjacent to a lighted passageway. While I normally sought a bunk in an area as dark as possible, I made an exception that night. I was not about to permit my cute little 18-year-old USMC rear end to be violated by a perverted squid.

Lousy Hygiene on Troop Ships

The many troop ships that to me to the various garden spots where I served were not exactly luxury liners. There were typically several hundred Marines in very cramped holds, with literally stacks of bunks that were often five high. We had to share our already tight bunks with all of our equipment. The air was thick with humidity, scent of gun oil, and body odors. Each Marine was given the opportunity for a unique shower about once a week: Thirty seconds of salt water to get wet, lather up, then another thirty seconds to rinse off! Without getting too graphic, most of us had a continuous "fishy" odor (and that is unfair to fish!).

My Vietnam Service (Not Much!)

In early 1964, I was one of several communicators from my battalion who were loaned to the 9th Marines Regimental Headquarters, the higher headquarters for three infantry battalions, of which my outfit was one. This headquarters had dual designation, and was also known as the 9th Marine Amphibious Force (9th MAF), with support responsibilities for any necessary deployment into the emerging global hot spot known as Vietnam. This loan was considered a pretty good deal, primarily because of the exceptionally good chow in the regimental mess hall.

For some reason, the only Marines in the mess hall were the actual cooks; all of the other duties, from cooking helpers to clean-up personnel, were performed by Okinawan contract personnel. Before being "loaned to regiment," I was among the many Marines who tried to sneak into this mess hall from time to time, but actually got to eat there when formally on loan to the 9th Marines/9th MAF.

From time to time, as a classified message courier, I shuttled classified material to and from the Danang Air Base in Vietnam, always on C-130 aircraft out of the Futuma Marine Corps Air Station, located just north of the Okinawa capital city of Naha. I spent a few nights, on several occasions, in a transient hut at Danang, but then shuttled right back to Okinawa.

During this era, there were occasional rocket attacks on the base, and ground combat was occurring, but the engaged Marines were exclusively performing as advisors to the South Vietnamese military.

These brief visits give me the right to say I served in Vietnam and that I am a Vietnam Veteran, but obviously my service was next to nothing. Because my trips to Vietnam were prior to March of 1965, I do not even rate the Vietnam Service Medal; instead, I added another star to the Armed Forces Expeditionary Medal that I received, along with the Marine Corps Expeditionary Medal which I had been presented for service during the Cuban Missile Crisis.

3rd Battalion, 9th Marines "Mounts Out"

Vietnam was starting to heat up, but the increasing role of the United States was still pretty much in a support and advisory status. My battalion, as part of the 9th Marine Amphibious Force, was in a constant state of readiness for deployment. In one instance, the battalion received the order to "mount-out" for deployment to Vietnam, and had packed up all the gear and was en-route to Kadena Air Force Base when the order was rescinded.

Exactly one month after the mount-out order, which had the precedence of a *FLASH* (an immediate emergency) message, the communications center copy of this now obsolete classified message was taken by Pfc John Kraus to the S&C (secret & confidential) files custodian, Sergeant Parmalee, for destruction. Sergeant Parmalee saw the flash designation and the day of the month, and immediately went into a panic, thinking that it was a brand new message to "mount out!" He rushed into the commanding officer,

Lieutenant Colonel W. F. Lane with what he mistakenly thought was a new emergency message. Colonel Lane was apparently influenced by the haste and excitement of Sergeant Parmalee and, assuming it was a new secret emergency mount-out, initiated the mobilization of the whole battalion!

Everyone again went into a high-speed wobble, packing gear, loading trucks, drawing weapons and all the other things associated with emergency mobilization. After about half an hour, the colonel apparently figured out what had occurred, (probably because other related messages were not coming down from higher headquarters), and canceled everything.

The shit hit the fan over this caper, and everybody pointed at everyone else for the misunderstanding. The colonel said his haste was based on Parmalee's excitement, and Parmalee said his haste was driven by the excited manner in which Kraus delivered the message to him, which was an absolute lie; Kraus just made a routine drop-off of obsolete messages. As the matter died down, Kraus was unfairly seen as the culprit, but all the key people pretty much just dropped the matter. For months afterwards, we all joked about the day when Kraus mounted-out the battalion.

Mom's Pearl Earrings

One day, right after payday, I took the bus from Camp Hansen to Koza, in order to buy my mom a set of pearl earrings from the Noritake Pearl Company, the top pearl jewelry outfit on the Island. First, however, I made my bi-monthly pilgrimage to the pawnshop outside the gate to get my electric razor out of hock, as I often pawned it a few days before getting paid! I got on the bus for the long ride to Koza, bought mom a very nice set of earrings, and took the bus back, exiting at the front gate to Camp Hansen.

As the bus disappeared down the dirt highway, I realized that I had left the bag with the earrings on the bus! I did something like slap my head in disgust, at which time I dropped the bag containing my electric razor, and watched it come out of the bag in several broken pieces! I then bent over to pick up what was left of my ruined razor, and in so doing ripped open the seat of my pants! Individually, these were three troubling events, but collectively they were kind of funny. As irritated as I was, I couldn't help but laugh.

Caught Sleeping on Watch – Kinda

Staying awake all night in a communications center can be pretty tough. This is especially difficult when you cannot really get much sleep during the day because of the constant noise and music and yelling in the barracks. One of the little ploys that I, (and probably millions of others), use to catnap was to sit at a desk with a book in front of me and my head resting in my hands, so it would appear that I was awake and reading a book.

I was using this ploy during the wee small hours of one of my shifts in the Communications Center at Camp Hansen on Okinawa when I became aware of someone standing in front of the desk where I was "reading." Though my hazy eyes I could see that the person was wearing gabardine trousers, which meant that the person was an officer. Thinking pretty quickly I chuckled as if I had just read something funny, then looked up straight into the eyes of the lieutenant who was the officer of the day! I said something such as "good morning sir, can I help you?" I will never forget the skeptical look on his face when he said something to the effect that I must be a very slow reader, because he had apparently been standing in front of me for quite some time before I looked up. I don't recall whatever response I provided before he left, but I was quite certain he knew that I had been sleeping and just chose not to make an issue out of it. Thanks, lieutenant!

A Most Unique Logbook Entry

Maintaining a log that reflected all that occurred during a duty shift in the Communications Center was mandatory. Each morning, the officer-in-charge would use that information for 24 hour situational awareness. On one overnight shift, when I was particularly tired, I really screwed up. After getting off shift and hitting the sack, the duty NCO (non-commissioned officer) woke me up, and said that the communications chief wanted me to report to him immediately. As I entered the Communications Center, he pointed to the logbook on the desk, and said, "what the fuck is this?" It turned out that in my exhausted state, my logbook entry was a combination of gibberish, thoughts to my family (as in a letter home), and indecipherable ramblings. I got my ass chewed out pretty well over that situation, but certainly learned a good lesson: don't create important official documents when exhausted.

Lieutenant Seitz Inspects The Crypto Vault – So He Thought!

Okinawa is a terribly hot and humid place during certain months, and can be downright miserable. The crypto vault and the colonel's office were the only air-conditioned rooms in the entire battalion, the former because of sensitive cryptographic machines. As one of the battalion's very few crypto specialists (in addition to my other duties), I was among the very few people who had access to this air-conditioned paradise.

One evening I was in the crypto vault when the officer-of-the-day, First Lieutenant Seitz, pounded on the door, demanding access; he mistakenly thought he had temporary access because he had the duty that evening. I diplomatically told him he did not have access, and urged him to review the access list posted on the door, a short list that did not identify his position. He clearly did not like my answer, and started quizzing me on just what I was doing in there, because it was after hours. Clearly, he was mad because I was a comfortable lance corporal and he was an uncomfortable lieutenant. He went so far as to suggest that I was in there just relaxing, reading, and enjoying the air conditioning! He demanded to know precisely what I was doing, and asked me to be specific about the tasks that I was performing. I politely told him that my duties were classified and that I was prohibited from divulging the information he demanded. He left in a huff, and I went back to relaxing, writing letters, and reading my book in the air-conditioned room.

"Keep Eating, You Will!"

Sick calls on troop ships reflect mass medical care at its worst. It usually consists of one or two enlisted Navy corpsmen, sometimes with the ship's physician, working in a tiny cubicle, tending to scores of Marines who are standing in a line that snakes throughout several adjacent passageways. The illnesses ranged from dripping male genitals to seasickness to open wounds, and everything in between. A percentage of the Marines are typically shitbirds seeking a medical slip to get out of a working party.

My friend, Larry, was concerned that he had not gone to the bathroom since the ship had left port, and thought it best to bring his condition to the attention of a doctor. He was in luck, because after waiting an hour or so in line, he found himself in the presence of the ship's doctor, and explained that seven days had passed since his last bowel movement, and that he felt he needed to have one.

Without laying a hand on Larry, no blood pressure exam or anything, the doctor said: "Keep eating, you will, next!" He kept eating, and he did.

Chapter Eleven
Marine Corps Air Station, El Toro
Station Communications

In June of 1964, after just under a year with 3/9, I was transferred to the Marine Corps Air Station, El Toro, just outside Santa Ana, in Orange County, California, thirty minutes south of Los Angeles. El Toro was the location of the 3rd Marine Air Wing. I was assigned to the Base Communications Center.

Humanitarian Transfer to MCAS El Toro

I actually rotated back to the United States a couple months earlier than scheduled. My brother wrote a letter to the Commandant of the Marine Corps requesting that I receive a humanitarian transfer to the El Toro Air Station, in order to be closer to my grieving mother in the aftermath of my pop's suicide. Frankly, he exaggerated the situation and a transfer to El Toro would be (was!) nice, but it was not really essential. Anyway, one morning on Okinawa, completely by surprise, I was told to pack my gear and get to the Port of Naha to board a ship that was leaving that afternoon! I dropped a quick note to my mom that I was coming home, but the letter and I were on the same ship! The first she got word was when I called from Pearl Harbor and told her I would be home in about a week. There was no time to write and tell the various girls I had been corresponding with that I was on my way home.

My 1958 Corvette

My big goal was to have a Corvette, and my wonderful mom helped me to achieve that task. While overseas, I put just about all of my money into an allotment to hopefully get a "Vette" when I returned to the States, and my mom put in considerable money as well. We had a plan and it worked like a charm. The cost of the car would be bad enough (for a low-paid enlisted Marine no less!), but the insurance for a teenager (even a "trained killer Marine!") would be near prohibitive for such a high-performance vehicle. My mom bought the car and paid a year of insurance in advance when I was still 7,000 miles away, and not considered in the rates, but it covered everyone in the household, which I then returned to!

It was a 1958 in classic red with the white scoop sides. I really loved that car, and certainly experienced the social benefits of having such a cool machine, but ended up selling it and getting a Volkswagen about a year later, because it just got too expensive to maintain.

Bye Bye Georgine

My sudden arrival back in the States came as a surprise to a lot of folks, one of whom was my favorite girlfriend, Vicki, who I immediately called. She was happy that I was home (well, she said she was!) and told me that her mom, whom I had known for several years, was hospitalized at the Santa Teresita Hospital in Duarte; she invited me to accompany her on a visit to see her mom.

Upon arrival, we entered her mom's room, which she was sharing with another woman, and the other gal was the mother of one of my other girlfriends, Georgine! I had dated Georgine before going overseas, was acquainted with her mother, and had maintained a romantic correspondence with Georgine while overseas, with alleged plans to get back together when I returned from overseas! The mother, and certainly Georgine, thought I was still on Okinawa, and here I turn up hand-in-hand with another girl in Duarte. Not good!

Georgine's mother never took those glaring eyes off of me; from the moment I entered until the moment I left the room. That was the end of Georgine.

Vicki's mom, Vivian, remains a dear friend. In writing this entry (March of 2009), I called and told her about the drama in that hospital room so many years ago. We had a good laugh. She remembered the other gal (Georgine's mom), and said that the issue of her being acquainted with me, or my infidelity, never came up.

Reporting In to Base Communications

Station Communications was part of the base's Headquarters & Headquarters Squadron, and was the communications center for all message traffic, classified and unclassified, into and out of the Marine Corps Air Station, El Toro. We processed all the messages that came and went from the various commands aboard the base. It was a critical and busy place. I was really somewhat of a fish out of water. Even through my primary MOS (military occupational specialty) was that of Teletype operator, I had neither the skill nor speed that was really needed for that place or the pace of operations, but was anxious to develop proficiency and do a good job. In the infantry, where I had previously been assigned, the teletypes were often not used, and speed was never a factor; in the "grunts" (infantry) I spent much of the time working outside of my MOS as either a field wireman or field radio operator. At El Toro, there were no foxholes and several women Marines; both of which were among the new concepts for Lance Corporal Bushey!

16 Hours on and 56 Hours Off

What a deal! I could not believe my good fortune. Except when scheduled for training or a medical appointment, we worked all night every third night, and were off duty the rest of the time! The sixteen- hours shifts were tough, from 1600 in the afternoon until 0800 the next morning, but the three days off were great. I went on "comrats" (communicated rations), which allowed me to live at home and purchase my meals (not much money, but still a good deal).

"No Doze" Was No Good

The schedule where I only worked every three nights started out pretty good, but after a few months became a real problem for my system. I have never been very good at attempting to get some sleep during the day when I have slept the night before, in preparation to work an all night shift; so I got little or no sleep during the day prior to my sixteen-hour shift. Then, at the end of the shift, the Sun had come up, and I was somewhat revitalized and as a result stayed up all day. As an unintended consequence, over a period of several months, I was getting about a third less sleep than I needed, and it was starting to take a toll on me. I was becoming somewhat of a zombie at work!

Then I discovered an over-the-counter medication, "No Doze," to help stay awake, and that made me an even more bizarre zombie. There was no chance for catnaps at work, because the volume of message traffic was very high, and getting ever greater as Vietnam was really heating up. Try typing messages on a Teletype machine when you are sleep- deprived and taking "No Doze!" Circumstances ultimately solved the problem when our shifts were reconfigured and the "16-56" was eliminated.

Station Communications – A Rough Beginning

The difference between an infantry communications center and air station communications center are like night and day. In the infantry, the equipment is portable, slow, often breaks, is frequently not used, and a great percentage of time is spent in the field. In an air station, the pace is always high, typing speeds need to be high, the equipment is fast and automated, the environment is sterile, and there is much less tolerance for error and weak performance. I did not do well initially. My typing speed was slow and my accuracy was low, and others usually had to pick up the slack and/or correct my work.

There was an initial honeymoon period where everyone was nice and tolerant, and realized that these were new skills for me, but there reached a point when people were expecting me to become proficient and it was not happening. Then, seemingly out of the blue, after I had been there four of five months, everything started going well and my skills lurched to where they needed to be, and maybe even a little beyond. Thank goodness! This was a good lesson that I believed has served me well in my patience and tolerance of others in situations where difficult skills are being developed.

Making Corporal – Being An NCO Was A Big Thing!

A pretty neat thing happened to me in early 1965: I was promoted to the rank of corporal. In one fell swoop, I was now a non-commissioned officer. This was a pretty big deal, as I was now actually addressed as "Corporal Bushey" by all my superiors, because of the traditional respect and expectations that went along with the rank. Most of my former peers didn't always use my title, but it was obvious that the relationship had changed. My friends were still my friends, but everyone realized that a non-commissioned officer had responsibilities that outweighed friendships, and there was clear deference to my rank when duties were performed.

In addition to putting new stripes on all of my uniforms, I also had the coveted red "blood" stripe added to the outer seam of my dress blue trousers, which was especially satisfying because I had the honor of wearing the dress blues that my brother had worn as a Marine in the 1950s.

My new exalted position did not prevent those of equal or higher rank from "pinning on my stripes," by slugging me in the arm (where the chevrons are placed) as I walked through the gauntlet of well-wishers, once in each direction so that each participant could slug both arms. My arms were pretty sore for several days, but there were no complaints from me. That was a well-recognized tradition and I was pleased to be a participant, especially since I was the one that got promoted.

The Sanctity of "NCO Country"

Becoming an NCO had a benefit that for me was enormous; I got to move into the coveted area at one end of the squad bay (barracks) that was reserved for corporals and sergeants. This sacred area was cordoned off from the lower enlisted (privates through lance corporals) by a row of wall lockers, with a curtain covering the entryway. Having my very own single rack (no double bunks for us!) in "NCO Country" was a real status symbol. Even though I usually stayed at my home in Duarte, I occasionally stayed in that sacred territory.

Shoe Polish Accident in the Barracks

This was ugly! The commanding general was conducting a massive inspection of all aspects of his command. Included was the much-hated "junk on the bunk" where all Marines methodically and carefully and obsessively created a masterpiece of personal equipment on their racks. Although I did not live on the base, I had to bring all of my uniforms and equipment into the squadron open barracks and put my stuff on display on an empty bunk. In taking all my stuff, requiring several trips, from my car into the barracks, I was also carrying a bottle of liquid heel and sole enamel for last minute touches to my books and shoes. On the last trip, I dropped the bottle and black dye went all over the floor right in the middle of the barracks! Holy shit!

Everybody went crazy. An hour or so away from the big annual inspection and a massive dye stain in the middle of the squad bay! I went into high gear, with no shortage of people saying some truly awful things to me, and started cleaning, sopping up, and scrubbing, and scrubbing, and scrubbing the cement deck (floor) with a course brush. After twenty or so minutes, I got up most of the stain, but what I created was even worse. There had to be at least twenty layers of floor wax over the cement floor, and I had taken the area where the wax spilled down to the bare concrete. The result was a beautifully waxed floor in a very large squad bay with a sizable white bare spot in the middle of the giant room. Ugly is too kind a word to describe what I had caused!

During the inspection, the general obviously observed my creation and commented that the twenty or so layers of wax, (which had been accumulating for years, perhaps as far back as World War II), should be stripped so the rest of the deck looked as nice as the white circle!

On the following Thursday night, which was "field day," all lance corporals and below, (I was a corporal, so was not required to participant in unscrewing what I had caused), had to strip the years of accumulated wax off the deck of the *entire barracks* so that everything matched the area that I scrubbed to the bare concrete! The hostility towards me was intense with several people, but fortunately did not last as long as I thought it would.

From Nothing to an Immediate Row of Ribbons

Shortly after completing my third year on active duty as an enlisted Marine, I was told to report to Major R. L. Critz, who was the commanding officer of the Headquarters & Headquarters Squadron to which the Communications Center was attached. I was to be awarded the Good Conduct Medal. By this time, I had been overseas a couple of times and had been in a combat zone or two, but never received a campaign ribbon of any sort; it all changed that day.

Apparently, in preparation for the good conduct ceremony, somebody went through my record book and determined that I should have already been awarded the Marine Corps and Armed Forces Expeditionary Medals for the Cuban Missile Crisis deployment, and an additional award of the Armed Forces Expeditionary Medal for Vietnam deployments with the 9th Marine Expeditionary Brigade; (this consists of a star which is placed on the first Award).

After Major Critz awarded me the Good Conduct Medal, the sergeant major handed him the two additional medals which were also to be presented to me. Very cool! In those days, when Vietnam was just starting to heat up, it was very common, in fact the norm, for career Marines who entered the Corps after Korea, to only have a couple of ribbons; typically denoting the Good Conduct Medal and National Defense Service Medal, (called the "fire watch" award because just about everybody got one). When I went to work the next day, folks were surprised, (and I know envious), that I had a complete row of ribbons, with two of them representing overseas expeditionary service.

Horrible Tragedy on Saddleback Mountain

The base turned very solemn on a very bad day in June of 1965. Late the previous evening an Air Force C-135, (military version of a civilian Boeing 707), full of Marines en-route to Vietnam, crashed shortly after take-off, with a loss all of eighty-four personnel on board. The aircraft had only been airborne for a moment or so when it crashed near the top of the prominent mountain ridgeline above the base, known as "Saddleback" because that is what it resembled.

The next few days were very hectic as the remains were brought down and placed in a hangar, and hundreds of messages were generated. I had the unpleasant duty of generating messages to the relatives of the deceased men, to be delivered personally by a Marine officer close to their homes, telling of the tragedy and initiating transportation arrangements of the remains. As distasteful as my role was, it paled in comparison to the Marines who had the horrible task of trying to identify the bodies and, worse yet, to personally notify the families.

The Pilots Were Fortunate to Have Died?

I did not observe any of what I am about to describe, but I knew everything about the situation, as I was the communications specialist who sent and received all of the message traffic. (For whatever reason, this duty could only be performed by a non-commissioned officer, [NCO], and that was me). Two Marine officers, the pilot and the co-pilot, decided to take their wives and a civilian couple on a RON, (remain overnight), flight in their CH-46 Sea Knight helicopter. To say that such unauthorized passengers was a mortal sin was an understatement; this constituted extreme misconduct and any penalty for such actions would be determined by a courts-martial, with prison time and a dishonorable separation very likely. The two pilots, with their enlisted crew chief, took off from the Marine Corps Air Facility at Tustin, (part of El Toro, where all helicopter squadrons were located, and under the same Marine Air Wing [MAW] command, but about five miles away from the main base), and landed somewhere around Lancaster, where they picked up their wives and a civilian couple, (husband and wife).

Their flight plan was to the Marine Corps Cold Weather Training Base just outside of the city of Bridgeport, at about 9000 feet, high in the Sierra Nevada Mountains. Their scheme was to drop off their unauthorized passengers just short of the base, in a clearing that was close to a campground, proceed and park the helicopter at the Marine Base, and spend the evening with their wives and the other couple.

However, there was a problem: the helicopter crashed in the High Sierras and everyone, including all of the unauthorized passengers, was killed.

At Marine headquarters in Washington, the shit hit the fan, and splattered all the way to El Toro, and then into the helicopter squadron and the group that the dead pilots were assigned to. All of the next-of-kin notifications were sensitive and difficult, but that was nothing compared to the shit storm that was about to hit the 3rd Marine Air Wing, the Marine Air Group, and the Squadron, (which, as I recall, was HMM367). The JAG, (Judge Advocate General – i.e.: military lawyers), descended on the place, and everything was up for scrutiny, from levels of supervision, to command actions, training, guidance, accountability at every level and on every issue, etc. I'm not aware of the final outcome or toll in ruined or damaged careers, but knowing the Marine Corps' practice of rolling heads when something big goes sideways, I suspect a bunch of careers were placed into jeopardy.

At the time of this incident, just about everyone said that the pilots were fortunate to have died, because their fate if they had survived would have been pretty dismal. This is a good topic for discussion on issues such as suicide where death might seem preferable to worldly consequences. Let there be no doubt, life would have been pretty tough, at least for a couple of years, had these pilots survived; but they could have gotten through it. Certainly their USMC careers would have been over, with less than honorable discharges and possibly with some brig time, but they would still have had decades of life after that.

In my more senior years, I have found that it is the rare exception, rather than the rule, where people do not get back on their feet subsequent to horribly nasty situations. Suicides are truly a permanent solution to a temporary problem. While there were no suicides associated with this tragic incident, it seemed like a good opportunity to express my thoughts on the issue.

A Successful Enlistment – Why?

This particular entry has roots that go back to 1965 when one of the sergeants that I worked for, Jerry Jaworski, for some reason that I do not recall, took me aside and told me that I was not like most of the other Marines that worked for him, that I had more "going for me" than the others, and to not be negatively impacted by some of the less-stellar Marines that we both served with. With the benefit of clarity that stems from decades of hindsight, and with far more articulate terms than I would have used at the time, I would like to address Sergeant Jaworski's comments.

While self-serving to say, it is true that I had a very successful four-year enlistment in the Marine Corps, and left active duty with some pretty decent life skills. As I look back and reflect on what I did well, I would have to give the following reasons: I was not a rocket scientist nor did I have any extraordinary skills, but I always did my best. While not always volunteering for additional tasks, I again did my best and did not gripe when they were given to me. I did not avail myself of the service of prostitutes, whether overseas or in the states. Notwithstanding a few beers now and then, I did not hang out in bars. I spent most of my free time, and there is plenty of it for Marines when not in the field, in relatively wholesome ways such as *Judo* lessons, correspondence courses, and organized base activities. I very seldom stayed out late, and even though liberty usually expired at midnight while overseas, I was usually in the rack when the lights went out at 2200 hours, and unlike many others was not a zombie the next day for lack of sleep.

While there were people I liked and respected, I always kept my own counsel and did not fall under the spell of any one person or group of persons. While there were certainly superiors that I did not think highly of, I showed them respect and did not engage in behaviors, like many others, that caused them to recognize my reservations about them. I wrote letters home and to friends, and left the Corps with some reasonable writing skills that were far beyond what I entered with. I worked on my education, and although the extensive correspondence course that I took (fingerprinting and criminal identification) yielded skills that I never used, it did keep me out of bars and occupied in a wholesome way. Finally, I went out of my way to get along with just about everyone.

Released From Active Duty

My schedule date to be released from active duty, at the completion of four years of active service, was November 12, 1965, which also was my twenty-first birthday. However, because I had been accepted at Citrus College, I had been approved for an early release from active to occur on August 20, 1965.

However, a couple of bad things happened on Friday, August 13, 1965 ("Friday the 13th!") First, the infamous Watts Riots began. Secondly, and even worse for me personally, the Secretary Of Defense, because of the escalating war in Vietnam and the need for personnel, extended all enlistments by four months, and also canceled all "school cuts," effective the day mine was supposed to occur!

I went into a state of rage and depression; the Corps had been a great experience, but I wanted out and to start college and begin my law enforcement career. My remaining active service went from about seven days to seven months! I even went to the Marine chaplain. I did not get any help, but I think he gave me a small camouflaged Bible!

After three or four days, the extension order was modified to permit the discharge from active duty of those Marines who had already been approved for an educational early Release.

On August 20, 1965, Corporal Bushey became *Mister* Bushey and drove rather unceremoniously out the front gate of the Marine Corps Air Station, El Toro. As was required, I reported to the nearest reserve center to update my address for recall, as I still had a two-year reserve obligation, (no meetings were required); I went to the artillery battery in Pico Rivera and checked-in, declining the opportunity to join that outfit as the communications chief. As I left active duty, the best way to describe my attitude is that I would not have taken a million dollars for my experiences, nor would I have paid a dime to do them over. Had someone told me that I would return to the Marine Corps, especially as a commissioned officer, I would have suggested they take a drug test.

Chapter Twelve
POST ENLISTED SERVICE AND CIVILIAN JOBS

Just Waiting to Turn ~~Age~~ 21 Years ~~of Age~~

Because I had been accepted at a college, the Marine Corps granted me an "early out" and I was released from active duty just before the beginning of the fall semester in 1965. For awhile it appeared that I would not get the early release as the Marine Corps extended all enlistments for four months as it was really ramping up for Vietnam, but it was ultimately determined that since I had already been accepted for a college that I would be released. I stayed pretty busy with school, which started three of so weeks after I got out of the Corps, and with a couple of jobs as well.

City of Hope Medical Center

My full-time job was working in the Cardiac Research Section of the City of Hope Medical Center as a research assistant and animal attendant. I worked for a great married couple that were also both very talented research scientists. There was much experimentation done on animals, primarily dogs, and it was my job to care for the animals to ensure they were healthy and properly cared for. I assisted in the surgical procedures involving the animals. It was very interesting and worthwhile work. The animals were treated extremely well and never suffered at all. Several years later an animal rights group broke into the animal research center, stole all the animals, and did thousands of dollars worth of damage. It was my honor and privilege to be part of such professional and humane research that no doubt contributed greatly to the medical body of knowledge that saved so many lives. Later, as a cop, I dealt with some animal rights zealots and found them to be strange and troubling people.

Pasadena Ambulance Company

I was in a four-wheel drive club that had intended to be a search and rescue team (never happened), and for that reason I took several first aid courses in Pasadena: basic, advanced, and instructor. The instructor for all these courses was the owner of an ambulance service in Pasadena, Bob Johnson (pseudonym). Bob had just bought the ambulance and sick room supply business from an old institution in Pasadena, which had originally been a mortuary and ambulance service (in that era, most ambulances were affiliated with a mortuary). Bob was a very decent guy and he offered me a part time job as an ambulance attendant, which I immediately accepted. Although Pasadena had its own ambulance service, Bob's outfit was one of two companies that provided city backup. Most of our work was transporting elderly and non-emergencies, but we did get a share of emergency calls as well. I really enjoyed the job, except for the sick room supply side when I had to wrestle very heavy and big oxygen cylinders up three flights of stairs for an emphysema patient who was waiting impatiently with a cigarette in hand!

Because of mannerisms, it was obvious to me that Bob was a homosexual, and pretty much the first person that I had a friendship with who was gay. He was a very decent and caring man, and someone with whom I had a great relationship up until his death in about 2002. Interestingly, Bob met and married a wonderful woman, who had a son, and Bob functioned as a great dad and husband right up until his death. I am certain that his wife, who also became a nice friend, was aware of his orientation; they made it work and work well for both of them and their son. Rest in peace my good friend.

Los Angeles County Sheriff's Department

Several days after reaching my 21st birthday, having previously applied and passed all the necessary hurdles, I was sworn in as a reserve deputy sheriff for the County of Los Angeles. I had a scheme to overcome the height restriction and it apparently worked, but then turned out to be unnecessary. The height requirement for deputy sheriff was 5'8" but I was a quarter inch short. It was a fact that the reserve physicians who administered the reserve deputy physicals were lenient on this requirement and occasionally permitted shorter fellows to slip through the process. My scheme was to become a reserve deputy based on the height leniency of a reserve physician, and then have that physical examination hopefully used when I transitioned to regular status. While I did in fact have another physical, I assume that my status as a reserve deputy tilted the scale in my favor, as I became an "off-the-street" deputy, assigned to the Biscaluz Center Jail, awaiting the next regular academy class.

I had previously applied to the Los Angeles Police Department, but was somewhat leaning towards remaining with the Sheriff's Department when told that I would not be in the imminent Sheriff's Academy class, but would be attending the next one several months later. When I went home the day of the bad news about the delayed Sheriff's academy, my certification to be hired by the Los Angeles Police Department was in the mailbox! After ensuring that I was in fact going to be hired by the LAPD, I dragged my feet until Friday, January 28, 1966, at which time I resigned from the Sheriff's Department.

Los Angeles Police Department

On January 31, 1966, at the Police Academy in Elysian Park, I was sworn in as a Los Angeles policeman. Off the 110 or so [hundred or so] young men who started that day, eighty-six [86] of us graduated three months later. Although a high school drop-out (but with my GED!), I must have acquired some academic skills in the Marine Corps, as I was rated 7th academically out of the 86 graduates in the Academy. Upon graduation, I was assigned as a probationary patrol officer in Central Division, which was just about all of the Downtown area. At the time, I was a member of the Individual Ready Reserve (IRR), with absolutely no desire to return in any form to the Marine Corps. However, within a couple of years, especially with Vietnam really heating up, I had pangs of guilt because many of my pals were still serving and I was not; I also harbored a continuing love and fascination for the Marine Corps. Those thoughts simmered for several years, and came to fruition subsequent to my chance encounter with a person who became a dear friend and Marine Corps mentor, Tom Vetter.

Private David Bushey. Co "B," 1st Gas Regiment, Edgewood Arsenal, Maryland 1919 - My dad.

Duarte High School, 1962, one of the few days I attended, just before entering the Marine Corps.

Pfc. David Bushey, Field Music School, MCRD San Diego, California 1951

Pfc. David Bushey (left), Marine Barracks, Treasure Island (San Francisco), 1951. This picture appeared on the front cover of Leatherneck Magazine, July 1951 - My brother

Platoon 290 – 1961-62, Marine Corps Recruit Depot – San Diego, California. L-R Private Keith Bushey (Left Guide), SSgt A. P. Jennings, SSgt B. R. Rawlings, Cpl B. R. Carlton, and Private Ed Hopkins (Right Guide). Both Bushey and Hopkins later became commissioned officers.

Camp Pendleton 1962

Infantry training. Camp Pendleton 1962

Infantry Training Camp Pendleton 1962

Message Center, Camp San Mateo 1962

Camp San Mateo 1962

With a pal, Dean Glanzman (left), and my 1952 Ford Crestline Victoria, Camp Pendleton, California 1962.

Camp Pendleton 1962

In the field, Camp Pendleton, California 1962.

Me on the left, and my good buddy Larry Schaetzel, eating "C" rations, Twenty-Nine Palms, California 1962.

United States Armed Forces Institute
MADISON, WISCONSIN

This is to certify that

BUSHEY KEITH D

has successfully completed the USAFI
TESTS OF GENERAL EDUCATIONAL DEVELOPMENT
HIGH SCHOOL LEVEL

this date 08 MO.   62 YR.   *service no.* 1989579

C. D. FOREMAN, Capt., USMC
COMMANDING OFFICER

Wilbur L. Brothers
WILBUR L. BROTHERS
ACTING DIRECTOR

DETAILS CONCERNING THIS CERTIFICATE ARE PRINTED ON REVERSE

After two years of high school, that I rarely attended, earning mostly D's and F's, I still don't know how I passed the GED Examination!

Outside the Message Center in the field, Guantanamo Bay, Cuba. Cuban Missile Crisis. October 1962.

My "Hooch," Guantanamo Bay Cuba, 1962

Waikiki Beach, July 1963

Camp Fuji, Japan 1963

Message Center, Camp Hansen, Okinawa 1963

As a lieutenant colonel, while visiting Okinawa in 1991, standing on the spot where I stood in formation as a young Marine, on November 22nd, 1963, when the unit was told of President Kennedy's assassination.

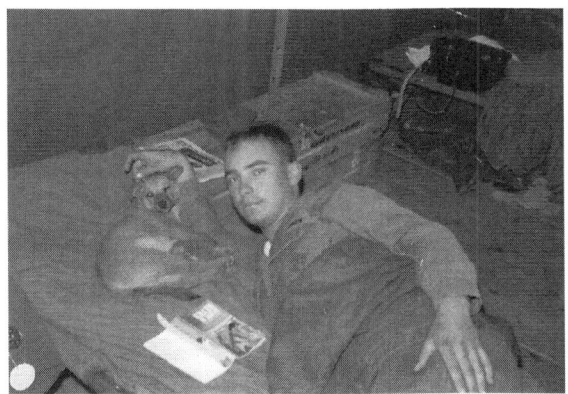

A nice dog, a warm sleeping bag, and a good book. Camp Fuji, Japan 1963.

On a troop ship with my pals during one of many voyages as an enlisted Marine.

Getting ready for liberty, Camp Fuji, Japan 1963

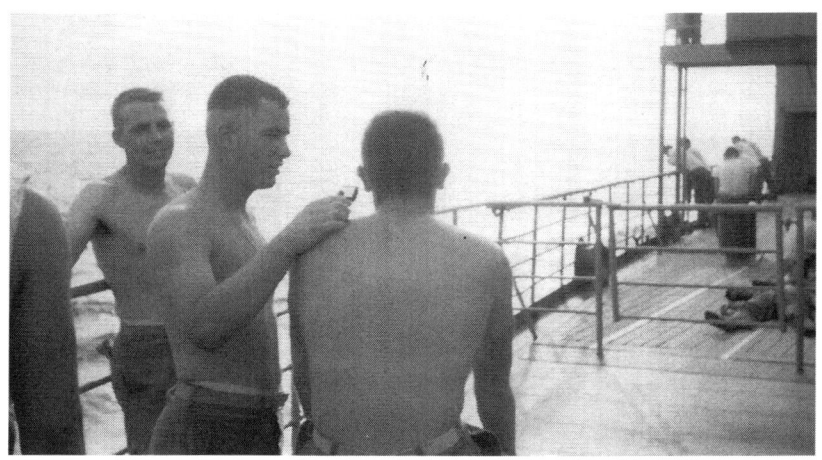
Giving a pal a haircut, on a troop transport, somewhere in the Far East 1963.

Enjoying a cigar while on liberty. Kin Village, Okinawa 1964

My barracks (right) at Camp Hansen, Okinawa 1963-64

Okinawa 1964

Parachutists, who in civilian life, were Los Angeles Police Officers (LAPD) Top L-R, Joe Mueller, Ernie Munoz, Jim Dunn. Bottom L-R, Jay Hernando and Keith Bushey. 3D ANGLICO 1

#D ANGLICO recruiting function circa 1974. L-R Capt. Bushey, SSgt. Taylor, Cpl. Keating, Pfc Wendy, Lt.Col. Clarchick, Capt. Palmer, and Maj. Mediavilla

3D ANGLICO Mess Night circa 1975, L-R, Capt. Zimmerman, Lt.Col. Rast, Maj. Beard (USA), Capt. Bushey, Maj. Parker, and Maj. Mediavilla

Exercise in the Chocolate Mountains circa summer 1975

Capt. Keith Bushey and Major Bud Harper. Coordinating a REDEYE Missile Launch. 4th FAAD. 29 Palms, California circa 1978.

Coordinating a REDEYE Missile Launch 4th FAAD 29 Palms, California circa 1978.

Coordinating a REDEYE Missile Launch from the roof of my personal vehicle that was painted the same colors as a range control vehicle that I often took into the field at 29 Palms circa 1978.

MASS 4 Marine Corps Ball with my daughter Stacy circa 1986

OP CRAMPTON, Marine Corps Base, 29 Palms circa 1980

Major Keith Bushey circa 1984

Senior Air Director, Direct Air Control Center, Marine Air Support Squadron Four. Marine Air-Ground Combat Center, 29 Palms, California circa 1983

Crapped Out in the shade. OP CRAMPTON. 29 Pals, California circa 1987

29 Palms
or
Twentynine Palms

Either we use the one that best fits

My first parachute jump upon returning to 3D ANGLICO as the commanding officer, July 1989. This photo appeared along with an article about me personally in the Leatherneck Magazine, March 1990

With a Japanese Self-Defense Force staff officer. Camp Chotise, Japan, joint exercise, January 1991.

Boarding a C-130 Transport, Japan 1991.

In the cockpit of a C-130 over the Sea of Japan, January 1991.

With a Japanese Self-Defense Force Staff Officer. Camp Chotise, January 1991.

Being briefed by Japanese officers during a joint exercise.
Camp Chotise, Japan, January 1991.

As the commanding officer of 3D ANGLICO, showing my new active duty ID card, reflecting a one-year assignment to active duty for the Gulf War.

With Sgt.Maj. Trumbich preparing for a parachute jump. Los Alamitos, California 1991.

With two of my best friends then and now, Ray Sherrard and West May. Los Alamitos Reserve Base, California 1991.

In my office at Camp Del Mar aboard Camp Pendleton 1991

Clowning around with Sgt.Maj. Trumbich and Lt.Col. Wes May, Camp Del Mar 1991.

A gift from my troops! 3D ANGLICO. 29 Palms, California. 1991.

Posing with Cathy and the anti-aircraft gun captured by my unit during the liberation of Kuwait, 1991 Persian Gulf War.

Ceremony upon promotion to Colonel, New Orleans, Louisiana 1993

Colonel Bushey driving a Light Armored Vehicle, 29 Palms, California circa 1995

Returning to base camp after an exercise 29 Palms California circa 1995

OP CRAMPTON, Marine Corps Base, 29 Palms, California circa 1995

In the rear of a CH 53 helicopter over the California desert circa 1996

Camp Pendleton 1997

Colonel and Mrs. Cathy Bushey. Marine Corps Ball. New Orleans, Louisiana 1997

Assistant Chief of Staff G-3, 4th Marine Division, New Orleans, Louisiana 1997

Chapter Thirteen
BECOMING A COMMISSIONED OFFICER

Unique Path to Commissioned Service

With each year after I left active duty and joined the LAPD, the Marine Corps was slowly pulling me back! As I watched the news and all that was occurring in Vietnam, with emphasis on the actions of Marines, I became more and more nostalgic. One day, while an undercover policeman at Cal State LA, and in the registration line, I found myself standing next to a fellow who I instantly recognized, because of his demeanor, as a policeman or a Marine; turned out he was both! Tom Vetter was a Mustang (former enlisted) first lieutenant in the Marine Corps Reserve and a deputy with the Los Angeles County Sheriff's Department. He initially thought that I was the left wing radical that I appeared to be, but after a little careful verbal sparring, I told him that I was a former Marine and an undercover cop. We became fast friends; this meeting turned out to be an extremely important fork in the road.

He was the assistant leader of the 14th Counterintelligence Team (USMCR), and very much interested and in need of the information I was gathering in my police undercover assignment. Because of our friendship, and because I had enormous investigative latitude, I initiated several investigations in directions of critical interest to the Marine Corps, resulting in several arrests of servicemen that were stealing items from warehouses in San Diego, the prevention of some other crimes, and the curtailment of some subversive and un-American activities. The FBI and the active-duty counterintelligence folks were amazed and very curious as to just how a reserve counterintelligence team was able to develop such quality and comprehensive intelligence. As a consequence, I was invited to apply for a direct reserve commission as an investigations officer! I applied immediately, completed more forms, and wrote more statements, than I thought possible.

A couple of months after all of my paperwork hit Headquarters, U. S. Marine Corps, I got a call from the Office of the Commandant of the Marine Corps, informing me that my application had been approved, but asking that I write a letter asking that my commission be held in abeyance pending completion of my police undercover assignment. The Marine Corps really liked the intelligence I was developing, and wanted it to continue, but did not want to be in the position of having a Marine intelligence officer investigating civilians subversives. This made sense, and I wrote the letter asking for my commission to be held in abeyance. As I recall, I submitted my application for commissioning in early 1969 and, had the abeyance issue not arisen, I would have been commission-ed in approximately mid-1969; when the Vietnam War was going strong. I requested the abeyance be lifted in June 1970, when my undercover assignment was over, and received my orders to report for commissioning in August 1970; when U.S. participation in the war was being dramatically scaled back due to "Vietnamization," stemming from the actions of President Nixon to turn the prosecution of the war over to the South Vietnamese Armed Forces (turned out to be a disaster, resulting in the fall of the South Vietnamese government in 1975).

The New Second Lieutenant

On a summer day in August of 1970, and accompanied by my new wife Barbara, I reported to the Marine Corps Officer Selection Office at the Military Induction Center, 1031 South Broadway Street, Los Angeles, where I was sworn in as a second lieutenant of Marines! This was the same building where approximately nine years before I was sworn in as a private, on my 17th birthday. The passion and possibility of returning to Vietnam for a real tour of duty had pretty much diminished along with the diminishing role of our government. It was a very proud day, but came nowhere close to the pride that I felt when I graduated from boot camp as a meritorious private first class! Damn, I never thought I would make corporal, and now I was a genuine commissioned officer! My new serial number (officers had different numbers that began with the number "0") was 0115390. Note: Several years later each person's social security number became his or her service number, and service specific serial numbers ceased to exist.

At the time of my commissioning, I had "surfaced" from my LAPD undercover assignment and was newly assigned as a sergeant in the Rampart Patrol Division. I had actually remained in the Intelligence Division for several weeks where I wrote what I believe to have been the first manual on the conduct of undercover police subversive investigations. By today's standards, it was a pretty premature document. When I went undercover, I received absolutely no training, as nothing was available. I was the first person assigned undercover on college campuses in Los Angeles and learned a great deal about techniques that worked well, and other behaviors to be avoided, and hope that others later benefited from my experiences.

Officer Candidate School – Waived

Because of the unique nature of my commission, as a "specialist officer," and because of my prior enlisted service as a non-commissioned officer, I did not have to attend Officer Candidate School (OCS)! This was the type of strange commission that can only occur in the middle of a chaotic situation (when approved in 1969, such was the state of our military forces); people end up with all kinds of commissions, although the majority of them are temporary, and the recipients eventually revert back to enlisted grade. Even though my commission was of a specialized nature, it was unrestricted and permanent! To this day, I still think there may have been a mistake, and that it was not intended to be unrestricted. I am certainly glad that it was!

Officer's Basic School

Although OCS was waived, it was expected that I would attend the Officer's Basic Course at Quantico, or as an alternative enroll and successfully complete the very extensive and laborious basic school correspondence course. Since I was newly married and had just made sergeant on the LAPD and was doing well in my career, I really did not want to take a six-month leave of absence from the police department to attend the regular basic school course. I enrolled in the correspondence course. When the first batch of materials arrived, I couldn't believe the size of the gigantic box and all of the books! Anyway, I started the course and completed a few lessons, then decided to see if I could ask that this course be held in abeyance until I had more time to devote to it. I sent a nice letter asking that the course be put on hold, and got a nice letter of response saying that my studies were being placed in abeyance, and requesting that I notify them as soon as I was able to restart the course. That was in 1971, and I still have not requested to restart the course!

Throughout my Marine Corps career there was a belief and expectation that I had completed this course and while never being dishonest in what I said, I just let my various superiors believe that I had completed this course, just like every other officer. Realistically, my failure to take this course did create somewhat of a void in my knowledge of some things, but I was a pretty quick study and hastily read up in those areas when issues arose, and I did just fine.

As I promoted, the selection boards apparently never went back that far in my records, as everybody pretty much automatically attends OCS and the Basic School, and it is not something that even requires examination. Had the selection boards realized that I never completed the Basic School, it is almost certain that I would not have promoted beyond major. Not only did I promote all the way to full colonel, but actually served as the Assistant Chief of Staff for Operations (G-3) of an Infantry Division, and was personally commended by one of the commandants (Mundy) for my ground combat skills and knowledge. I beat out and promoted beyond a great many fine officers, some of them Naval Academy graduates, and all of them graduates of the Basic School, despite my failure to attend this course. I kept this secret to myself until the day I retired!

Chapter Fourteen
FOURTH LIGHT ANTI-AIR MISSILE BATTALION (4th LAAM)

In mid-1971, after a number of years of not being a member of a Marine Corps unit, I was joined to one of the "firing batteries": the 4th Light Anti-Air Missile Battalion. The battalion headquarters was in Fresno, California. The mission of the battalion was completely related to the ground-to-air HAWK medium-range missile system. As I recall, there were approximately 150 personnel assigned to the Pasadena reserve center at that time. In the LAPD, I remained assigned to the Rampart Patrol Division during my short tour with 4th LAAMBn.

My First Reserve Unit as an Officer

The Fourth Light Anti-Air Missile Battalion (4th LAAM) was my first reserve unit. I joined this outfit in September of 1971, at the recommendation of one of my police subordinates at the Rampart Division, Officer Bud Harper, a Vietnam Veteran who was then a first lieutenant in the Marine Corps Reserve and assigned to this outfit. I was in "Charlie" Company, located in Pasadena, and was assigned as the platoon commander of the Support Platoon.

The mission of 4th LAAMBn was to train and be prepared to deploy the ground-to-air HAWK Missile System. To attain proficiency and obtain the military occupational specialty for this field required about a year-long school at Ft. Bliss in Texas, and realistically was a skill I would not attain; that is why I was in the service platoon (motor transport, supply, communications, etc.) It was not my intention to stay in this unit for very long, and I didn't. It was a pleasant few months, especially having the opportunity to spend time with Bud Harper, who has become a dear and lifetime friend.

One negative aspect of this assignment was the fairly high number of lousy Marines in the unit who joined the reserves to beat the draft; by this time the draft had turned into a lottery and many fewer persons were being drafted, but those folks who previously joined to beat the draft still had a six-year reserve obligation. This was the beginning of a difficult period for the Corps, regular and reserve, as the transition to an all-volunteer military occurred. We had about ten or fifteen turds who resisted military haircuts, had lousy attitudes, and who spent most of their time trying to weasel out of their assigned tasks.

MGySgt Aretakis and 2ndLt Bushey Meet Again

Before this chance encounter, the last time I saw Pete Aretakis was in 1964 when he was a staff sergeant and the Communications Platoon chief at Camp Hanson on Okinawa, and I was a lance corporal. We bumped into each other at the commissary at Camp Pendleton, with me first recognizing him. To say that he was stunned to see that I was now an officer would be an understatement, but he appeared to be pleased and even a little proud that one of his men had joined the commissioned ranks. He was a master gunnery sergeant and had just returned from Vietnam, having served multiple tours and experiencing some pretty bad stuff. I graciously accepted his offer to be his guest for a cookout that evening at his home on base. We had a great and fun evening, and relived and laughed about many of our past experiences. The next time we met was again at Camp Pendleton, just after the first Gulf War in 1991, when I was a lieutenant colonel and he was a retiree on the way to the Golf Course! In about 2005, Pete made his transition to eternal life. RIP Pete.

Chapter Fifteen
14th COUNTERINTELLIGENCE TEAM

In January of 1972, after having spent only about four months in the 4th LAAM Battalion, I transferred into the 14th Counterintelligence Team, an entity of the 4th Marine Division, and co-located with the 4th Tank Battalion on the site of the historic WWII base, Camp Elliott, located just across Highway 395 from the Naval Air Station, Miramar, north of San Diego. The mission of the team was to train and be able to deploy a team of counterintelligence personnel, all either officers or non-commissioned officers, for the following mission: Using both active and passive measures, to deny the enemy valuable information about the friendly situation, and also countering hostile espionage, subversion, and terrorism. The team was small, and consisted of a total of approximately 15 persons. In the Police Department, I was assigned to the Rampart Division when I transferred to 14th CIT, but transferred within the LAPD to the Management Services Division about halfway through my counterintelligence assignment.

Transferring and Working Within My Military Occupational Specialty

I transferred to the 14th Counter-Intelligence Team (14th CIT) in early 1972. The unit was housed in the back of a WWII warehouse on the old Camp Elliott Marine Base, just west of Miramar Naval Air Station (now a Marine Corps Air Station) in San Diego. I enjoyed the unit, which was small, but did not particularly like the politics of the team. When I got there, the team was led my Major Fred Tschopp and, when he moved on, the next senior man, Captain Bill Addison (pseudonym) became the team chief, and immediately got rid of my good friend and mentor,
then-First Lieutenant Tom Vetter.

This was problematic because Bill was a captain on the Los Angeles County Sheriff's Department and Tom was transitioning from sergeant to lieutenant within the same agency. Bill was not in good graces with the sheriff at the time, Peter Pitchess, and took a leave of absence and went to Vietnam for a tour.

Upon returning, Tom helped Addison get into the 14th CIT, knowing full well that he was bringing in a person senior to him who would probably end up as the Team OIC, but felt it was the right thing to do. Addison was just too political, and spent an enormous amount of time hob-knobbing with the high-ranking Marine officials assigned to the higher headquarters. Addison then gave Tom Vetter, the person who brought him into the team, his walking papers! I remained in 14th CIT for a couple of years, and for the most part enjoyed the assignment. I made first lieutenant in late 1972 or early 1973.

"Slow Down Jack, This is God Speaking to You!"

As a young adult, I had a series of International Scout four-wheel drive vehicles, all of them full of radios, a winch, rescue equipment and – most of all – a very loud industrial public address (PA) system. About 4:30 on a Saturday morning, along a pitch-dark stretch of Interstate 5, somewhere south of Oceanside, while en-route to my Marine Corps drill in San Diego, I was presented with a wonderful opportunity to have some fun. There were only two cars on the road, mine and the one ahead of me, which I recognized as being driven by a fellow Marine who was also on his way to our drill. As we went around a curve, I turned my lights off and accelerated, and got just to his right rear, in his blind spot, where even if looking right in my direction he could not see me because of the darkness. I then turned on my public address system and said something like, "Slow down Jack!"

He was clearly startled, his brake lights went on, and he actually swerved a bit. It was hilarious watching him try to figure out where the voice was coming from, and I was naturally adjusting my speed and location so as to not be seen by him. A few moments later, I spoke to him again and said something about being God and watching over him. I finally put my lights back on, got alongside him, and said "good morning" over the PA. We got a good laugh out of this situation, and it was always fun listening to Jack as he told the story to others. I had a great deal of fun with the PA system!

Pandemonium in a Navy Bar in Norfolk

While in Norfolk working the Fleet Intelligence Center, another Marine Lieutenant and I decided to have lunch in a bar that also sold sandwiches, and had nude dancers on a "runway" in the center of the establishment. Except for Tom (my pal) and myself, every other patron was a sailor. As we were eating our sandwiches and drinking our beer, one of the strippers started demonstrating some truly sensuous "bumps and grinds" about one foot from our faces, most likely believing that a couple of Marine officers would have to maintain some degree of decorum – wrong. Tom lunged at the dancer's crotch as if he were going to take a bite out of her genitals! She screamed and fell backwards, but was caught by a sea of sailors. Everybody got a good laugh and the dancer learned a good lesson: Don't assume all Marine officers are gentlemen!

Fleet Intelligence Center – Atlantic

This was a most interesting and, at the time, highly classified experience. The 14th CIT was assigned to the Fleet Intelligence Center in the Naval Base in Norfolk, Virginia. We spent two weeks assembling, coordinating, matching, and evaluating data pertaining to military activities in various nations. What I remember most is that damn Tom Vetter; he worked all day, took a couple-hour nap after work, then went bar-hopping until around 0400, slept until about 0630, and started the process all over again! I kept up with him for about two days, and then threw in the towel and reverted back to the real me, a nice meal after work, a little TV, then eight hours of sleep.

Installation Intelligence School – Fort Meade, Maryland

This was a fairly interesting school, and helped us to sharpen the skills we used in doing physical security inspections of military facilities (for classified materials, spots of vulnerability, suspicious activities, etc.)

Upon arrival, we were placed in an old WWII barracks, where dividers had been added so as to be allegedly "suitable" for officers, but there was no air conditioning, and the *windows had been painted shut!* August in Maryland is incredibly hot and humid, and this was just plain miserable. I had an acquaintance nearby, a badge collector, who hooked me up with a fan. After prying open a couple of windows in my cubicle (tearing the hell out of the wooden frame), and directing the fan strategically, it was almost bearable.

Reestablishing My Roots in Pennsylvania

As a Marine officer, I made quite a few trips to the Washington (D.C.) area, and later as the LAPD liaison on Capitol Hill as well. During one of my first trips, I took a day off and drove to York, Pennsylvania, to see if I could find any Busheys. Boy, did I; the name was all over the place! Despite the name, I could not find anybody to talk to, but left my business card in a "Bushey mailbox."

I got a letter from Evelyn Bushey Miller, who identified herself as the unofficial Bushey family historian, asking me to tell her more about my heritage. Several days after sending her the information she requested, I got a nice letter back from her that started out with, "Welcome back into the family!" As it turned out, her part of the family had lost contact with my part of the family when my dad and his brothers came to California after World War I, and she was thrilled to have heard from me. That contact has resulted in several trips to the York, East Berlin, and Gettysburg area, including participating in a couple of Bushey family reunions.

Among my most memorable events have been several visits to my dad's home located at 134 East 5th Street in North York, which was built by my grandfather, Jacob Bushey. Different residents over the years have graciously allowed me to walk through the house, go down into the basement, and spend time on the porch. The house has been modified a bit, but is largely the same as when my dad and his family lived there.

The meadow immediately below the house is still there and still a place where kids play, including I am sure, the same low rocks that protrude here and there in that meadow. I have also visited but not entered another home, located at 809 West Princess Street, in York, where the family lived and where my grandfather operated his construction business. I never tire of visiting that area and reflecting on my heritage.

Crazy Marines and Perplexed CHP Officers

In 1972, on an extremely foggy morning while Tom Vetter and I were carpooling to San Diego for our Marine Corps drill meeting, I lost control of my small Toyota while trying unsuccessfully to make a last moment transition from one freeway to another. We left the pavement, went over a small curb, and bounced about forty feet down an ice plant-covered incline. Two California Highway Patrol officers were on-scene almost immediately.

As one of the officers yelled down to inquire if we were okay, Tom flashed his sheriff's badge and yelled something to the effect, "I am a sheriff, and this man just groped me, and that is why we crashed!" I immediately flashed my badge and yelled that I was an LAPD officer, and that the crash was caused because the sheriff grabbed me in an inappropriate manner! The two CHP officers just shook their heads, laughed, and said they were "out of here," or some similar term. As they departed, we asked them to send us a tow truck. Tom and I seldom fail to discuss this incident when we get together, and continue to laugh at the scene the CHP officers encountered that foggy morning.

"Gentlemen, Join Me at the Bar"

During my early years in the Marine Corps, both as an enlisted Marine and as an officer, social drinking was a major pastime to the point of being *de facto* required in many instances. As a second lieutenant, an invitation by your boss to "join him at the bar" or "join me at the club" might just as well have been a direct order. At the end of the day, the last thing that I wanted to do was go sit at a bar with an alcoholic captain or major so he had a captive audience for his bullshit stories. I tried to avoid this crap as often as I could, and in one instance I was "counseled" by a captain that I was expected to join him and a major for after-hour libations, and that a failure to do so could create a negative perception that could affect my fitness report! Nobody was happier than I when heavy social drinking went through a transition from near mandatory to near-career ending.

Fred Jones Brings Me a Navy Nurse

Fred Jones (pseudonym) was among a small group of officers with special skills in the field of installation security; he and the rest of us received occasional orders to conduct physical security evaluations (PSE's) at different Marine Corps commands. We were at the Naval Air Station in Alameda (California) inspecting the Marine Reserve CH-46 and A-4 squadrons when this unique incident occurred.

After chow, as had become our practice, I retired to my quarters and Fred, an absolute Marine Corps legend for his sexual escapades, headed for the Officer's Club for a night of booze and debauchery! At some point in the middle of the night, I was awakened by someone who was fondling me! It was a drunken Navy nurse who Fred enticed to visit me in my rack! It was very thoughtful of Fred, but I was more interested in sleep than the slobbering, drunken nurse, and I chased her off.

Jackie Larsen Goes Crazy

Retired Marine Master Sergeant Dennis Larsen (pseudonym), also a retired police motorcycle officer, is truly an unforgettable character. Men love him because he is so funny and entertaining; women hate him because he is sex-crazed and cheats on any female who has the poor judgment to hook up with him. The incident occurred during a weekend drill of the 14th CIT, when Dennis was a staff sergeant. Some of us had taken our wives, and we were staying in the Sands Motel, just outside the main gate of the Miramar Naval Air Station. As usual, Dennis, and another Marine, Staff Sergeant Roger Garza (pseudonym), were down there by themselves and had a couple of honeys in their motel room.

I was awakened in the middle of the night by a phone call from Jackie, Dennis' wife. She demanded to know where Dennis was and I told her that I did not know. She then asked if I would give him a message if I should happen to see him, to which I replied, "of course!" About as near as I can recall, the message went something like this: "Tell Dennis that I have his service revolver and that I am on my way down there to kill him and the bimbo he is with, and then I will kill myself!" I encouraged her not to do anything rash, but said I would pass on the message if I saw him. She hung up, and I immediately called his room. When he answered I could hear the tinkling of glasses and feminine giggling, and I gave him Jackie's message, to which he replied, "Oh f—k!" There was then an intercept from the motel operator with an emergency call for his room, which was obviously Jackie, and I said "bye bye Dennis." Within a minute, there were skidding sounds from the parking lot, indicating the high-speed departure of a vehicle.

We got the whole story the following morning. Jackie got through to Dennis and accused him of infidelity, and of course he denied everything and professed his love for her and no one else. She called him a liar and, with his police service revolver, started shooting up the detailed military models and artifacts in his den. She was shouting profanities at him over the phone, and describing the possessions of his that she was blasting, and he was hearing it all. A very panic-stricken Dennis Larsen, rushing home in an attempt to save his marriage and possessions, was driving the car that abruptly left the Sands.

Note: Jackie Larsen later committed suicide. I do not know if they were still married at the time.

Roger Garza Meets A "Real Woman" in New Orleans

Members of the counterintelligence team were attending a weekend of training in New Orleans, and a few of us went to the French Quarter to see the sights and have a beer. One of the other Marines was the aforementioned Staff Sergeant Roger Garza. As we entered this one bar, a truly pathetic creature, dressed as a female but obviously an ugly man, rushed towards Roger and screamed: "Mr. Garza, Mr. Garza, I am a real woman now!" I looked at Roger and he was smiling! Turns out that this person, who had just had a sex change, had been an inmate in the county jail where Roger had previously been assigned, and adored Roger because of his compassion in getting prompt medical attention for this person whose artificial breasts were knocked out of alignment during a jail fight some years earlier! It did not take us long to get out of there.

Note: Several years later, Chief Warrant Officer Roger Garza, as a sheriff's deputy, was fired for his role in a massive scandal of the Narcotics Squad. I do not recall Roger's role, but the overall investigation involved illegal searches, seizures, selling some of the dope they seized, lying, etc.

Chapter Sixteen
3D AIR-NAVAL GUNFIRE LIAISON COMPANY (3D ANGLICO)

In April of 1974, after having spent over two years in the 14th Counterintelligence Team, I transferred to the 3D* Air-Naval Gunfire Liaison Company (ANGLICO) in Long Beach, California. 3D ANGLICO is a subordinate unit of the 4th Marine Division. The mission of all ANGLICO companies is to provide continuous training so as to be able to provide personnel to either the U.S. Army or allied military organizations who are skilled in assisting other military organizations (beyond the USMC) in calling-in Marine close air support (CAS) and Naval Gunfire (NGF). In addition to the men in the platoons who possess these skills, doctrinally filled by commissioned officers, the company also has personnel in the support role as well (motor transport, clerical, communications, parachute riggers, etc).

Since airborne insertion is a major method of entering theatres of operations, especially when in support of U. S. Army airborne divisions, the majority of the personnel on-call in CAS and NGF are airborne qualified. As I recall, there were about 200 men in the company at that time. (ANGLICO is one of two company-sized organizations in the Marine Corps that is commanded by a lieutenant colonel, the other being force recon). At that time, the unit was located in a turn-of-the-century old school house and compound under the Vincent Thomas Bridge in Wilmington.

Within the Police Department, at the time I transferred into 3D ANGLICO, I was a sergeant assigned as the officer-in-charge of the Manuals & Orders Unit within the Management Services Division at Parker Center (police headquarters). A couple of years later, while still in 3D ANGLICO, I was promoted ~~within the Police Department~~ to the rank of lieutenant and served temporarily in both Communications and Hollywood Divisions ~~before~~ *Prior to* my regular assignment to the Hollenbeck Patrol Division.

*Note: "3D" is the Marine designation for 3rd for the ANGLICO community.

Most Likely Hired by Mistake!

After a couple of years in the 14th Counterintelligence Team, I decided to seek a transfer to the 3D Air Naval Gunfire Liaison Company (ANGLICO), in Long Beach. It was a very desirable unit,

(This is the same info. you provided in the first paragraph of this page. Although 3D ANGLICO consider revising)

with a mission to insert Marine forward observers into forward tactical positions with Army or allied military personnel, and to act as forward observers to assist others in acquiring Naval Gunfire or Marine Close Air Support. Operational personnel, both enlisted and officers, were required to be jump (parachutist) qualified. This mission really appealed to me, as did becoming jump qualified.

However, I was hired based on a mistaken belief that I was a qualified administrative officer, which was not accurate. There were a lot of short cuts during the Vietnam War, and I was one of them. Although commissioned because of my skills and knowledge in the area of counterintelligence, I could not be formally assigned that military occupational specialty (0210) because it was a "hard MOS" that could not be assigned without attending a six-month formal school. Instead I was commissioned as an investigations officer (0170). An administrative officer typically has an MOS in the 01— series. When I applied for 3D ANGLICO, they took one look at my MOS and mistakenly concluded that I had the ability to perform the skills in the vacant administrative billet that desperately needed to be filled. After several months of completely screwing up the admin office, the mistake was recognized and I transferred to one of the operational platoons. This was a very fortunate mistaken fork in my many roads!

A Forty-Year Prank by a Stoic Military Physician

Prior to attending parachute school, I first had to successfully pass a very rigorous physical examination to ensure that I was qualified for the rigors of jump training. This physical was conducted at the Armed Forces Examining Station in Los Angeles, where most of those being examined were new enlistees. The doctor was a crusty old fart who was marginally pleasant. When he looked in my right ear, he announced that I had a big build-up of wax, then he threw what I assumed was a big plug of wax, larger than I could have imagined, into the trash container, and it landed with a clearly audible thump. Then he repeated the process and made the same comment on my other ear, concluding with another plug of wax and another audible thump. I was astonished at such a buildup of wax that the debris from my ear would make a loud thump, especially because I try to keep my ears clean. It wasn't until just a year or so ago that a light went off in my brain-housing group and I realized that nothing legitimate could have come out of my ear that would have landed with such a loud thump! That crusty old fart pulled a good one over on me that lasted for about forty years.

155

A Painful Meeting With a Deceased Staff Sergeant's Next of Kin

Like many reserve officers, my responsibilities have always been such that some duties require being physically present at the reserve center not just on drill weekends, but often during the week as well. On one such visit the inspector-instructor, a regular lieutenant colonel, asked if I would accompany him to the home of a staff sergeant who had been killed in action in Vietnam (the war was still being waged at the time, although the drawback of U. S. Troops was well underway), and whose remains had just been located and returned to the states. We had the medals and decorations that he had been awarded, plus the flag that covered his casket when his remains were transported. Our visit was not well received at all. The woman screamed at us, badly scorned the Marine Corps and the United States, called us killers and pawns in President Nixon's war, knocked the flag and medals out of my colleague's hands, and ordered us off her property. Dealing with the pain of a badly grieving mother was not a pleasant experience, and unfortunately was not an isolated experience for those men who were often called upon to make these types of casualty calls.

Jump School (Parachute Training) at Fort Benning, Georgia

Upon joining the unit, I started getting myself in physical condition for jump school. I finally got my orders to report to the Airborne Course at Fort Benning, Georgia, a three-week school that went from early June to July 3rd, 1974. It was very hot and humid, but I truly enjoyed the training. The physical aspects were pretty tough, and of the roughly 650 persons who took the qualifying physical fitness test, only about 425 passed it and continued with the training!

In addition to the regular attendees such as Marines, Navy SEALs, and soldiers assigned to airborne duty, there were large numbers of Annapolis midshipmen and West Point cadets, as well as NROTC students, attending as part of their summer training. The first week was fitness training, the second week was practicing from towers and other training devices, and the third week was the actual jumping to achieve the five qualifying jumps necessary to be awarded the coveted airborne badge.

Could Jump, But Could Not Walk at Fort Benning!

On Monday of "Jump Week," my first and second actual jumps were just fine. During my third jump on Tuesday, I sprained my ankle a bit. On my fourth jump on Tuesday, I really aggravated my ankle and could hardly walk. The Army "Black Hat" first sergeant called me aside and inquired about my injury, to which I downplayed the matter and said I would be fine the next day. In no uncertain words, he said that he believed my injury was probably more serious than I was describing, and he directed me to report to him the next morning for evaluation before I would be permitted to make my final qualifying jump. Truthfully, I was really hurting and was afraid I would have to be dropped (one day and one jump short of graduation!)

Another Marine officer, 2ndLt Dave Jacobson, had just graduated from Annapolis where he had been on the gymnastics team, and he had the answer. I had befriended him and took him under my wing upon starting the course, and boy did he reciprocate in a big way! He told me of a midshipman who competed successfully in a gymnastics meet with two broken ankles, and was going to use the same treatment on me.

That night, we soaked my foot in ice for as long as I could take it (very painful!), and did this several times. I got up a couple of hours early the next morning and kept my foot under very hot water for about half an hour. Then, Dave wrapped my foot so tight that I could hardly feel it. We then walked the couple of miles to Lawson Field where we were to draw our equipment and board the aircraft for our final jump. Walking was difficult at first, but became easier as we went along, and pretty soon I was doing great, with not the slightest limp!

I reported as directed to the First Sergeant for evaluation, and he couldn't believe the jumping jacks that I performed, commenting that my recovery was miraculous; he good naturedly chased me off when I commented that Marines heal faster than soldiers. Anyway, we went up for the last and fifth jump and it was great – not a pain or a glitch. After the jump we went to some bleachers, were awarded our wings, and then returned to our quarters to pack our gear.

When I removed my boot and the wrapping, I could not walk without assistance! I had to be helped out of my quarters to transportation, and also in boarding the commercial flight home. I had a virtual black band of broken capillaries stretching horizontally around my foot, and could not walk normally for almost a month! Thank you Lieutenant Jacobson!

Where Did All the Kids Go?

This situation could have been beyond horrible. Early in my tenure with 3D ANGLICO I held the additional responsibility of recruiting officer. I took this job seriously and actually orchestrated several large outings of recruiting prospects, and "poolees," (sworn into the USMC, but awaiting orders to basic training), to Camp Pendleton. It was a great recruiting event, as we let the kids actually stand adjacent to the drop zone as the parachutists descended. We had thirty or forty kids on a drop zone and I had left for just a few minutes to grab several cases of C-Rations; when I returned all the kids were gone, and I did not pass any vehicles on the road.

When I asked where the kids were, one of the Marines pointed to a pair of CH-46 helicopters disappearing over the horizon! This violated every military regulation and federal law that ever existed, and was a very bad thing. For whatever reason, someone thought it was okay and told the helicopter pilots that transporting the youngsters via military aircraft had been authorized. Thank God there was not an accident. The end of my military career would probably have been among the lesser consequences of dead or injured kids.

"What the Hell is a Utility Pass?"

This is the kind of mischief that can occur when people understand the system, especially a Mustang Officer. In the early 1970s it was a mortal sin to wear the utility uniform off the base. It was common for people to drive to a base in civilian clothing, then pull off into the bushes and change into the utility uniform. Although my primary duty was that of an airborne fire support coordination officer, I had the additional duty of being the command's recruiting officer, and as such spent a considerable amount of time working with recruiters and coordinating visits by recruiting prospects to Camp Pendleton.

I had an idea to address the constant switching back and forth from utilities to civilian clothes: making a "Utility Pass." In my LAPD assignment, I worked in an office that had a machine that could make letterheads and identification cards, and had my secretary make up a very official looking card, with a massive Marine Corps emblem in the background, that read across the top: UNITED STATES MARINE CORPS UTILITY PASS. She made up several of these for me and my two enlisted assistants, with all kinds of verbiage and other information typically found on things such as identification cards and driver's licenses. To give myself a little cover in case things went sideways, and to create a scintilla of legitimacy, I took the three passes to my commanding officer for his signature in the space that was provided. He said he had never heard of such a thing and I confessed to just making them up; he thought it was a good idea and signed them.

I used them for a couple of years, as did my two enlisted assistants, (also LAPD officers: Emmett Badar and Chuck Hawley). Finally, one afternoon when departing Camp Pendleton, we were stopped as always by the gate guard and told we could not depart in the utility uniform, and as always we displayed the Utility Passes and were waved through the gate. As we were driving away the Sergeant of the Guard ran out of the guard shack and yelled to his enlisted subordinate not to let us leave in utilities, to which the guard yelled back that it was okay because we had Utility Passes. As we pulled further away and approach the highway the last thing we heard was the Sergeant of the Guard yelling: "What the hell is a Utility Pass? I still see Emmett and Chuck from time to time and we always reminisce and laugh over our Utility Passes.

An Unsurvivable Malfunction – Or So I Thought

During one of the five mandatory final jumps at Fort Benning, I observed a parachute malfunction that I did not think anyone could survive. While on the ground gathering my chute after landing, I heard the "black hats" (instructors) yelling through megaphones at one of the other jumpers that he was going to be okay, and to get his feet and knees together.

I looked up and couldn't believe my eyes; a soldier had a double malfunction with his reserve chute and main chute both tangled together in what was referred to as a "cigarette roll." He was descending at a very high rate of speed, passing the other descending jumpers as if they were sitting still.

I knew that he was a dead man and felt that the verbalization from the "black hats" was intended to let him think that he had a chance - beats knowing that you are going to die! Not wanting to see the death, I turned my head away just before he hit the ground, but sure felt the impact when he hit.

Obviously, people rushed to him, just in case there was anything that could be done. About five minutes later, the guy was on his feet and shaking out his chutes! For all of us on the drop zone that day, this was an unbelievable vivid lesson that a well-executed parachute-landing fall (PLF) can mean the difference between life and death. As I write this entry, I am sixty-seven years old and experiencing the aches and pains that stem from an active life; this guy had to have had some back trauma that would eventually be troublesome.

Gold Wings and a Bloody Chest

All parachutists from all branches of the military go through the one military jump school, run by the Army at Fort Benning, Georgia. Upon completion, each graduate is awarded silver basic parachutist wings. An additional five jumps, while in an authorized jump billet and representing some additional skills (night jump and equipment jump) are required before a Marine is awarded the Navy-Marine Corps Parachutist Insignia, which is gold in color and similar to pilot's wings.

For years, an absolute ritual and rite of passage was for the senior jumpers, without regards to rank, to "pin" the wings on the new jumper's chest by vigorously slamming the wings, with no clutches on the rear pins, into the man's chest! With each hard slam into the chest, and as blood clearly becomes apparent, the new jumper typically yells "U-Rah" to demonstrate toughness and glee at finally getting his "blood wings!" It was also common for jumpers to put their bloody undershirts in frames and display them in their workspaces. This practice was officially prohibited, I think in the late 1970s, but realistically continued, just in somewhat of a covert manner.

Subsequent to a big scandal over "blood wings" in the mid-1990s, the then Commandant of the Marine Corps, General Krulak, issued a edict not only strongly prohibiting the practice, but also proclaiming that it had never been a tradition or accepted practice. At the time of this assertion that "blood winging" had never been a tradition, I was a colonel and working for a general who, when he was a captain and I was a lieutenant, was among the many senior jumpers who slammed my wings into my chest! I was and continue to be troubled by General Krulak's inaccurate remarks; he was a good man, but knowingly declaring that a past practice or military tradition, (however crude or primitive civilians might perceive it to be), never existed, detracted from his credibility, at least with me.

Spectators Go Wild at El Toro Parachute Jump

My "Cherry Jump" (first jump after jump school) was beyond memorable. We jumped at an air show at the Marine Corps Air Station in El Toro, California, which has since been deactivated and no longer exists. We jumped from an R4D, which was very old and the military version of the DC3, also known as the C-117D and a World War II workhorse.

One of the other jumpers had a malfunction with his main chute and had to deploy his reserve, and with his razor-sharp K-Bar knife cut away part of the tangled main. The truly amazing factor was that we were jumping from about 1,200 feet, and had a descent time of only about 60 seconds!! The crowd went wild with applause, and I cannot imagine that the jumper didn't have to change his underwear. This kind of stuff, so I thought, only happens in movies, and the cutting away of static lines in such a short time just did not seem possible, but it happened and I was among the witnesses. This jump was personally painful for me because I landed on the concrete runway instead of the intended grassy area, and as with a few other jumps ended up limping for a few days.

A Catering Truck of Marine Field Gear!

In preparation for a big inspection, as I recall a "CG" (Commanding General's Inspection), the commanding officer ordered an inventory to ensure that all personnel had all of their 782 Gear (web and related gear for field activities). The results were horrible! Scores of Marines were missing one or more items. Even though most of the missing items were not of a critical nature, they were required and their absence would cause the unit to fail a major portion of the inspection. The procedure for replacement was a "missing gear statement" of each Marine, a statement of endorsement and a recommendation from an investigating officer (loss through negligence or at no fault of the Marine), and then submission of the package up through the chain of command – a real pain and administrative burden. As was not unusual, the commanding officer, Lieutenant Colonel Howard Rast, turned to me for an expedited solution (actually, I may have initiated a recommended solution).

I contacted a surplus store in Los Angeles which had all items in serviceable condition, negotiated reasonable prices, and had them bring a truck full of all needed items to the next drill. At the beginning of the next drill, every Marine who had missing gear, upon being paid (this was before direct deposit), was shuttled across the freeway to the Long Beach Naval Station to cash their drill check. Then shuttled back to the unit where, based on the inventory sheet I had developed, purchased the item(s) they were missing from the surplus vendor. Within four hours, our unit went from missing scores of items to each Marine having 100 percent of his gear! Not a very conventional operation, possibly never done before (in such an organized manner), and maybe even of borderline legality, but it worked. I put a great premium on this type of creativity, and am proud of my role in activities of this nature. You can make an enlisted man an officer, but that lance corporal mentality is still there!

Not in Long Binh, or in Long Beach

When hired into 3D ANGLICO, the commanding officer mistakenly thought that I was an administrative officer, because my military occupational specialty was 0170, and he desperately needed someone with those skills. I should have corrected him and explained that my specialty was "investigations officers," which was in the 01—series, which is the administrative series, but I knew I probably would not have been able to get into the unit otherwise, so decided to see if I could BS my way as an admin' officer! It went okay until we had an inspection from one of the higher headquarters.

The rules say that pistol and rifle qualification scores have to be typed on the appropriate page in each Marine's record book, which I thought was stupid because it meant literally disassembling each folder in order to remove the weapon's qualification page, in order to type the scores in the designated space. I directed the clerks to cease the practice of removing and typing on the pages, and gave direction that it was okay to neatly write the scores in ink, and then I would validate the scores with my signature, saving a ton of time.

When the big inspection occurred, the inspector was a Mustang captain who had spent his entire career as an admin weenie, and did not think much of my shortcut. He exclaimed that "we didn't do that in Long Binh (Vietnam) and we are not going to do that in Long Beach!" After this inspection, the commanding officer – who by this time kinda liked me – permitted me to transfer to one of the operational brigade platoons.

Two Corporals Meet Again – As Gunny and a Captain

In the mid-1970s, I made a trip to the Marine Corps Supply Center in Barstow, California. I went to the Supply Section to see about getting the newly released camouflage utility uniforms issued to my personnel. I lingered at the counter as the supply sergeant was chatting with another gunnery sergeant, then noticed that the gunny had a familiar tattoo that I had seen before; it was a man, Doug Bowden, that I had worked with at the El Toro Station Communications Center in 1965, where we were both corporals. He and I had been good pals because he was living with a gal, Linda, who, like me, lived in Duarte, and we often car-pooled to and from the base. He was shocked that I was a captain, and we had a great visit. He had married Linda and they were living on the base.

I went back a month or so later and the three of us had dinner and a nice visit. Our friendship had a sad ending when Linda committed suicide a couple of years after Doug retired. Doug had a drinking problem, but the Marine Corps kept it from getting too bad; however, once retired he had no need to be sober on a regular basis, and soon followed Linda by taking his own life.

Major Brady Parker

Major Brady Parker (pseudonym) was truly a unique personality; one of those folks who you would probably want to have at your side in combat, but problematic and troublesome the rest of the time. He had a motto: "always marry an ugly woman and she will never leave you!" He married an ugly woman, had a beautiful daughter, and then the ugly woman took the beautiful daughter and left him!

When I first met him, he noticed that the zipper catch on my brand new leather flight jacket (a very hard-to-get and prestigious item) was broken, and he volunteered to take it and get it fixed. The next time I saw it was a year later; he was wearing it and it was worn to hell! Then, he decided to apply for LAPD so I had my wife make a great dinner for his arrival and overnight stay before his oral interview the next day, and he did not arrive until almost midnight! When he did arrive, before hitting the sack he asked if we had a cigarette; we had a very large bowl full of C-Ration cigarette packages arrayed in a decorative manner, and Barbara told him to help himself; when he left the next morning we discovered that he took every one of the packages (probably 50-60 packages). The last I heard of him was when he snatched his daughter from the front yard of his former wife's home and disappeared. I have often wondered what became of old Brady, and know that it could not have been a happy ending.

Scrounging Equipment at Fort Irwin and Major Mendoza

As a captain, I was the officer-in-charge of an ANGLICO Detachment to Fort Irwin in support of an Army exercise, BRAVESHIELD XVIII. At this time, circa 1977, 3D ANGLICO was in pretty sad shape with much of our equipment, especially motor vehicles, deadlined (out of service) for lack of replacement parts, and radios that we couldn't use because the budget was not adequate to acquired the minimum numbers of batteries we needed. My scrounging and innovative skills really paid off with respect to what I was able to come up with during the exercise, a trait that was further enhanced because the Army actually "writes off" materials as having been expendable during the military maneuvers. This is contrary to the Marine Corps, which has strict accountability for everything.

I scrounged so much stuff that we had to have an additional large truck (6X6) respond to Fort Irwin to help get all the goodies back to Long Beach. Among the things that I scrounged for the unit were: a pallet of radio batteries, enough canvas to replace the worn and torn canvas on all of our trucks and Jeeps, spare rear-ends and transmissions beyond what we needed, a score of cots, and dozens and dozens of the most often used motor vehicle maintenance parts. Additionally, I had a badly damaged Jeep towed to Fort Irwin and it was completely repaired by the 7th Infantry Division field repair facility!

I was proud at what I had done for the unit, but the Inspector-Instructor, Major Tony Mendoza (pseudonym), was not. I kept getting the word that he was telling others that I acted inappropriately and unethically in my massive acquisitions, which was not true; I knew my stuff and how to get things done without violating the rules (at least not too many of the rules!) My commanding officer, Lieutenant Colonel Howard Rast, and the assistant inspector-instructor, Dave Zimmerman, both thought that I had done well.

I finally got tired of the back channel back stabbing by Mendoza and asked for an audience with him, in the presence of both Rast and Zimmerman. At the meeting, I threw down the gauntlet and said that I wanted to tell him everything that I did, how I did it, and why I did it, and at the end wanted him to either stand-up and thank me, or call the Naval Criminal Investigative Service, (NCIS), and initiate an investigation into my actions. At the end of my presentation, he stood up and thanked me! Mendoza was a decent enough fellow but somewhat of a "Nervous Nellie." Not just because they backed me, but for many reasons related to their behavior in this matter, Howard Rast and Dave Zimmerman were two of the finest Marines that I had the good fortune to serve with.

Lieutenant Hopkins? Captain Bushey?

In the late 1970s I made several trips to the Barstow Marine Corps Supply Center to provide training to the military police personnel. The MP chief, a gunnery sergeant, was a pal and I was doing it as a favor to him. Early one morning I was having a cup of coffee with some of the guys when a familiar looking second lieutenant came into the Quonset hut. It was a fellow I had gone through boot camp with, Ed Hopkins! As a recruit, he had eight years of prior military service, four each in the Navy and Air Force, (and in the former was a corpsman with the Marine Corps in the Korean War). Not surprisingly, he was both the platoon and company honor man.

In our recruit graduation photo, he as the right guide was seated on one side of the drill instructors, and I as the left guide sat on their other side. I was not surprised that he was commissioned, as a limited duty officer in some type of logistics specialty. I think he was surprised that I was a captain, but we had a great visit that morning, and also got together for lunch again a few weeks later. I regret that I have lost contact with Ed, as he is not in any of the typical USMC databases. I hope he is doing well.

Major Mendoza and the Hovering Huey at Big Bear

For one of the weekend drills, I led a detachment of parachutists to Big Bear, California, for joint parachute operations. We conducted the drill in conjunction with an Army Reserve Special Forces unit that provided Huey helicopters and parachutes. It was a great opportunity as the Army folks brought scores of extra packed 'chutes and all of us got in quite a few jumps.

Major Mendoza (pseudonym), a regular Marine assigned to the unit, came along and brought his girlfriend. At the time I owned a two-story home right alongside the airport at Big Bear, with a large upstairs bedroom where one entire wall was a large open window with *no shades or curtains*. Since it would not have been right for me to sleep in my house while the troops slept in the bush, I stayed with the troops at night and let Mendoza and his honey use my home.

Early the next morning, we coaxed one of the pilots to fly over to my house and hover right outside the large upstairs bedroom window where Mendoza and his honey were sleeping. The pilot keep us in stitches with his version of Mendoza's antics in covering himself and his girlfriend, shaking his fist, and moving his lips in what had to be some truly offensive profanities.

Chocolate Mountains Gunnery Range – A Real Garden Spot!

The Marine Corps has some real garden spots for training, and one of them is the truly humble mountain range known as the Chocolate Mountains, located midway between Yuma, Arizona, and El Centro, California. It has been used as a military gunnery range since World War II, with decades of ordnance being dropped as part of aerial bombing practice.

In the late 1970s, in the middle of the Summer, I was part of a detachment that spent two weeks on a barren mountaintop serving as a forward observer in coordinating close air support and bombing missions for Navy and Marine Corps pilots flying out of the Marine Corps Air Stations in Yuma (Arizona) and El Toro (California), as well as some flying from aircraft carriers off the coast of California. It was hotter than hell and a constant battle to stay hydrated. At night, we camped along the All-American Canal at the base of the mountain and spent quite a bit of time in the water as refuge from even the night heat. We later learned that some folks, close to the Mexican border, had illegally dumped raw sewage in the canal, those things floating past that looked like turds apparently *were* turds!

Bad Conduct Discharge and Humiliation for a Malingerer

Lieutenant Colonel Bill Toole is a great Marine and a no-nonsense individual who was the commanding officer of 3D ANGLICO when this incident occurred. There were several Marine reservists who were less than worthless, and just stopped coming to the weekend drills. We processed several of these men for discharges but, when their bad conduct discharges arrived, had trouble just getting them to come to the reserve center so we could process them out of the Corps.

Toole had an idea, and he tried it on a turd whom I will call Private Worthless. We had one of the low-ranking clerks call Worthless and tell him there were a couple of old drill paychecks waiting for him, and to drop by and pick them up. Worthless was as stupid as he was useless, and he promptly came by. While Private Worthless was in the office waiting for his "checks," Toole had the entire outfit of several hundred men, and a few women, fall into formation.

Worthless was then lured outside, at which time Lt.Col Toole ordered Worthless to "front and center" in front of the entire formation. LtCol Toole then read the discharge out loud to all assembled, ordered the entire outfit to "about -face" (so everybody was facing away from Worthless), then loudly ordered Worthless to leave the compound, stating that he gave the about face order so that good Marines would not have to look at him. Worthless, in his gang attire of baggy tan pants and oversized flannel shirt just slithered away. This action was clearly outside the norm of acceptable command behavior, but we all thought it was just fine. Bill Toole, who to this day remains a dear friend and fellow member of the Devil Pups Board of Directors, was a bit unorthodox at times, but in my judgment always in good and appropriate ways.

Holy Shit, I've Just Torched Camp Pendleton!

These twenty or so minutes of fright and despair had to have taken a year off my life! During a training exercise at Camp Pendleton, I was the senior man on a CH-46 helicopter that was transporting a bunch of Marines to the Case Springs area of Camp Pendleton, located high in the Cleveland National Forest.
As the helicopter descended into a landing, I authorized the "popping of smoke," with a colored smoke grenade, to assist the

pilot in evaluating the winds. The smoke grenade immediately started a fire, and the high winds pushed the flames clearly beyond our ability to control or exting-uish. I just knew that the inferno would spread throughout the base, potentially race into adjacent civilian communities (Fallbrook, San Clemente, etc.), that my career was over, and that my "careless" actions could well result in enormous liability for both the USMC and me.

I immediately contacted "Long Rifle" (range control), gave a situation report, direction of the flames, and requested the dispatch of fire apparatus. I evacuated all of our people, and sat there sweating bullets as I awaited the arrival of fire-fighting assets.

After about forty-five minutes, with no fire apparatus anywhere in sight, I re-contacted range control to ensure assets were en-route and was told that there would be no response. When I asked why there was no response, range control advised me something to the effect that such fires occur all the time and that they are permitted to just burn themselves out, and to not be concerned! That was among the sweetest radio transmissions that I had every received.

Slippery "Little Bugger" in Virginia

This was a funny situation involving a Southern Belle who was as pretty as a picture and as dumb as a rock. Four for five of us Marine officers were having dinner at a restaurant in rural Virginia and one of my colleagues was trying to make time with this very pretty gal. After clearly indicating that she was not interested, she suddenly took notice of his nickname embroidered on his shirt, which was different from his first name. Her face lit up like a Christmas tree and, in a southern accent you could cut with a knife, she exclaimed, almost verbatim: "Why you slippery little buggar, you are an intelligence officer, you can't fool me, of course I will go out with you!" He took her hand and they walked off to whatever destiny was to be theirs. We all looked at each other in amazement, as we were not in the intelligence field and had no idea what caused this gal to arrive at her conclusion, but for the sake of our colleague we were glad that she felt such was the case!

Chapter Seventeen
4th FOURTH FORWARD AREA AIR-DEFENSE BATTALION (4th FAAD)

In April of 1978, after four years in 3D ANGLICO, I transferred to the 4th Forward Area Air Defense Battalion in Pasadena. This was primarily a "ground" unit, but was under the command of the 4th Marine Air Wing. The mission was to train and, if necessary, deploy Marines who were trained in the employment of the REDEYE Ground-to-Air Missile System. As I recall, there were about 200 Marines assigned to the unit, of all ranks. In the Police Department, I had several assignments during my tenure in 4th FAAD, including serving as a lieutenant in Central Traffic and Rampart Divisions, and after promoting to Captain in both the North Hollywood and Hollywood Field Services (Patrol) Divisions.

Reasons for Transferring to Pasadena

During this era, there was a rule that an officer could only remain in a reserve unit for three years, with the possibility of a one-year extension, and then had to go elsewhere. I had been in 3D ANGLICO for about four years and it was time to move on. My good pal, then Major Bud Harper, whom I served with on the LAPD, invited me to join the 4th Forward Area Air Defense Battalion (FAAD), as his executive officer for the battery that he commanded, at the Reserve Center in Pasadena. My old pal Tom Vetter was at the Pasadena Reserve Center also, but he was in a HAWK Missile Battery, and he encouraged me to transfer to Pasadena as well. I really liked ANGLICO, and enjoyed jumping (parachutist), but my tour was over and Pasadena was pretty close to my home. I remained in Pasadena for about four years and although overall enjoying every command I was ever part of, FAAD was not among my favorite assignments.

A "Good Old Boy" Outfit

More so than any other outfit that I was part of, the Marines at the reserve Unit in Pasadena, for the most part, spent their entire careers in Pasadena. It was truly a family-type of outfit, with many close friendships among the officers and staff non-commissioned officers. In my judgment, this was not a healthy situation, and occasionally led to decisions based on tenure and friendships as opposed to competency and other military considerations. The following situations illustrate my concerns.

Staff Sergeant Jones (not his real name) was a very nice man who spent his entire career in Pasadena. As a platoon sergeant, he was an absolute failure, and was unable to perform the most rudimentary tasks in personnel and equipment accountability. He was also very gentle and soft-spoken, and had no credibility with the troops. I "encouraged" him to transfer to another unit in hopes that he could gain the skills elsewhere that he failed to develop in Pasadena. My actions in causing him to move on were not well received by some of the other more senior people.

Gunnery Sergeant Lawson (not his real name) was also a nice and decent man who likewise spent his entire career in Pasadena. He was the battery gunnery sergeant, and pretty much scatter-brained in much of what he did. In civilian life, he was a security guard and had never even developed the skill to operate a motor vehicle, (instead having to depend on buses to get around). Without suggesting that being a guard is a bad thing, or the inability to drive a car is a bad thing, they represent life activities that are pretty much inconsistent with the demeanor and activities of a senior Marine staff non-commissioned officer. He eventually moved on to another unit, and I can only hope that there was an improvement in his personal skills.

Chief Warrant Officer Tom Ramirez (pseudonym) had been in Pasadena since his return from Vietnam as a corporal. He was the long-time commander of the service platoon (comm., motor transport, supply, etc.) I felt that he should attend the three-week school to learn the REDEYE Missile System so that he would have the critical skills that might be necessary if we were to be activated and a need arose in the firing battery, a contingency that made perfectly good sense, and which was easily accomplished. He fought me tooth and nail and never did attend the short and simple course that would have greatly expanded his skills and value to the Marine Corps. He liked the job that he did, liked the latitude he enjoyed with a variety of summer training opportunities, and had little sympathy for the best interests of the Corps. He badly resented my unsuccessful efforts to send him to the REDEYE course.

Whining Nurse Shuts Down School in Alabama

In the late 1970s I was among the Marine officers who were selected to attend the reserve course of the Air Force's Air Command & Staff College in Montgomery, Alabama. All in all, it was a great course.

Most of the instructors were Vietnam fighter and bomber jocks that really knew their stuff. I actually drove to and from Alabama, and took Jake with me. He farted around the quarters during the day, and rode his bicycle (I took in the van) around the base. During this time I was also very active as amateur radio operator ("ham") and worked a lot of high frequency stuff.

One day a very troubling event occurred. The day consisted primarily of listening to really good presentations in an auditorium, then breaking up into small groups, going into seminar rooms, and discussing the details of the presentation that we had just heard. Included among approximately 300 officers from all branches were about a dozen Air Force nurses. In the middle of a really good presentation, it was obvious that someone on the side of the stage was motioning for the presenter to step to the side, which he did and then disappeared.

The lights came on and a full colonel stepped to the microphone and apologized for the alleged inappropriate remark that the presenter, an Air Force major, had just made! None of us could think of anything inappropriate or off-color that the major said, but the whole show came to a stop because of a complaint made by one of the nurses. We were all asked to make statements about what we had heard, and I think most of the folks agreed with me that we could think of nothing that was said that was inappropriate. I don't know how the matter turned out, but it struck me as a pretty sorry state of affairs when one person with a questionable objection can bring an entire auditorium to a halt. I think it was an unfortunate overreaction on the part of the colonel.

Keith and Jake Visit Streator, Illinois

Streator was among the cities that my mom lived in as a young girl, and a place that I heard a lot about, from both my mom and my grandfather, as I was growing up. Having driven to the Air Force Staff & Command College in Alabama, Jake and I decided to drive back on a path that took us through Streator. Upon arrival, I looked in the telephone book and found the name of a lady who was a niece of my grandfather, Arch Hood. She was very nice and gracious, and showed us around the town.

While much had changed, I found a few places where I know my grandfather was prominent, including the local Masonic Lodge. Unfortunately, due to the closing of a large company, which like many Midwestern towns was a big part of the community's lifeblood, the city was in decline. My mom, to whom I spoke on the phone when we got there, could not remember where the house that she lived in was located. She did recall the park that she played in as a little girl, and we went there for a few minutes of reflection. We did not really know her very well, and as time went on lost contact with the nice lady and shirttail relative that hosted us that enjoyable day.

Mediterranean Cruise

Shortly after joining FAAD, I was the officer-in-charge of our participation in an amphibious exercise in Sardinia. The detachment flew commercial to Cherry Point, the military C-141 to Barcelona, Spain where we boarded the USS Inchon (LSD-12), and spent two weeks with an infantry battalion out of Camp Lejeune, North Carolina. We had a day of liberty in Barcelona, another day in Toulon (France), and then conducted an amphibious exercise in two Sardinian cities, Dechmonte and Campidano. Then another day in Madrid, where we were not able to leave the Air Force Base, and the flight back to Cherry Point and then home.

I served as the battalion's S-3 alpha (operations section), and pretty much enjoyed the experience. The people in Spain were overall nice and friendly, and just about everyone I encountered in France, including those at the police station I visited, were arrogant jerks. My experience in France validated all the bad things that I had heard about the arrogance of the French people in general; I have no desire to ever again visit France. I know that the majority of French people must be cordial and decent, but my experiences have not been good.

The Bogus Conscientious Objector

We had a slug in the unit who claimed that he needed to be discharged from the Marine Corps because he was a Jehovah's Witness and therefore a conscientious objector (CO). I was assigned to investigate the validity of his claim and make a recommendation regarding his application for a CO discharge. My irritation at this idiot caused my vindictiveness and creativity to go into high gear.

I went to a Jehovah Witness church in Pasadena (that was not the location where he was allegedly attending services), obtained basic written material about the church, and developed a high quality fifty word multiple-choice test on that religion. For the date of the interview with this so-called pacifist and his attorney, I also asked two pastors from the same church to come to the reserve center, interview the idiot, and give me their assessment as to the genuine nature of his conscientious objector claim.

He and his attorney were stunned at the process that I had assembled, especially the test, but he had no choice but to follow my orders and instruction. Despite the very simple and basic nature of the questions, he blew the majority of the questions.

After the interview with the two pastors, the one that appeared to be in charge made the following statement to the assembled group: "We do believe that he is sincere as a conscientious objector, but he has a long ways to go before he will ever be a Jehovah's Witness!" It was my pleasure to recommend denial of his request, and to certify that in my judgment his claim was bogus. Fortunately, my boss ignored my vindictiveness, rejected my recommendation, and processed the idiot out of the Marine Corps. My boss was right in ridding the Corps of that worthless person.

The Alcoholic Inspector–Instructor Moves In

About a year after my assignment to Pasadena, Major Ron Arnold (pseudonym), a regular Marine officer, was assigned to Pasadena as the inspector-instructor. He drank more than he should have, and was always strapped for money, no doubt because of a recent divorce and child support payments. He quietly moved into a storeroom at the Reserve Center, which was a big no-no because he was drawing pay for quarters; he got caught by the battalion commander and was told to vacate the room immediately or face disciplinary action.

He and I chatted and agreed that he would move into a vacant room at my home in Azusa for a reasonable monthly sum. This was not a very good deal, and he never paid me a cent! He took advantage of me because of his position, and because his actions were likely to have a favorable impact on my Marine Corps career, including selecting the next commanding officer (who he made clear was going to be me), I just kept my mouth shut and he lived rent-free for about three years, all the while drawing a pretty good stipend each month for his housing allowance.

Ron was never in particularly good graces with higher headquarters and, about four months before the old commanding officer's tour was over and the new commanding officer was to be selected (thought to be me), he was transferred. It was clear that the new inspector-instructor came in with some marching orders to clear certain things up, and that he did not think fondly of Ron Arnold, quite understandably. It was good that he was finally gone, because I, too, had my reservations about his personal and professional qualities. It was personally not in my best interests because Ron's advocacy for me did not set well with his replacement, and I was tainted by the association, and although the clear likely choice, I was not selected as the new commanding officer when the incumbent's tour expired.

This was one of life's unfair experiences; I had no choice but to tolerate this leech as he took advantage of me for a couple of years, and then I was tainted and suffered professionally because of the association! However, I must say that in the end I came out ahead. Had I been selected at the commanding officer of the unit, I most likely would have remained in the anti-air field and not have gone onto the military path that was to be mine as a field-grade officer. The path that resulted was far better than the path that I unsuccessfully sought in Pasadena.

A Hooker Takes My Picture in Barcelona

This was funny. I was fascinated at the ornate nature of an old hotel that had been the Nazi headquarters during World War II, and was in the process of taking a picture of it when a woman, obviously a prostitute, asked if I would like her to take a picture of me standing in front of this historical location. I appreciated and accepted her offer. As I was standing and having my picture taken by the hooker, another lieutenant from LAPD and his wife, obviously on vacation, came around the corner and saw me standing there and obviously associating with a prostitute. He smiled and kept on walking. For years after that, my denials that I was having anything done beyond the photo fell on deaf ears with that fellow.

Fond and Grateful Thoughts for a Disabled Vehicle

It's funny the things that we remember and some of the thoughts that we had. I was a real fan of the Scout 4X4 vehicles that were produced in the 1960s and 1970s by the International Harvester Corporation; in fact I had three of them over the years. Because of a fondness for the earlier models, around 1978 I bought a used 1966 model as my third such vehicle. It served me very well on a number of trips, and especially in the backcountry during my periods working for the Department of Fish & Game.

Somewhere around 1981, while en-route home from my USMCR reserve meeting in Pasadena, the engine blew up! It was ugly, with horrible sounds, smoke, and an instantly dead engine. Nevertheless, I was able to coast graciously to the side of the freeway and my old Scout took its last breath and stopped right in front of an emergency callbox! Honestly, my consternation over my predicament was far exceeded by my appreciation for a vehicle that served me well right up until the very end.

Chief Corpsman Livid Over New Urine Test Procedures

This was really funny! I have long had the ability to make extemporaneous presentations in a way that makes it appear that I am reading what I am saying verbatim from a document. This has served me well on numerous occasions, especially in the making of public and military appearances. It has also enabled me to have a great deal of fun over the years, such as grossing out the Navy chief petty officer that was the unit's senior corpsman.

A minor directive of some sort dealing with random urine testing for drugs had just come out, and I saw the opportunity for some fun. I took it to the chief, and feigning disbelief, read "verbatim" the new rules for the role of Navy corpsmen in obtaining urine samples, to include the mandatory physical handling of each Marine's private parts to ensure that there was no hidden small tube that might contain someone else's "clean" urine that a drug abuser could substitute as his own during a drug test.

The chief got very upset, with the veins popping out in his neck, his face got red, and he launched into a tirade about how he had now seen everything, and how he would retire before being forced to manhandle (pun intended) the genitals of all the Marines in the unit.

We all got a big kick out of this, especially because of the chief's near-violent reaction; it took him quite awhile to settle down and see the humor in my actions.

"Cruise Control" is NOT "Automatic Pilot!"

When I first arrived at Fort Bliss, there was a big buzz going around the base about the foolish actions of some well-heeled foreign students. Fort Bliss was a major facility for training military students from allied counties in a variety of different skills, so much so that there is actually a German Luftwaffe command right there in the middle of the Texas desert. Among the many foreign students there were fairly large numbers of military personnel from the oil-rich Middle Eastern countries whom we were friendly with, and most of them came to the United States with quite a bit of money.

It seems like one of these rocket scientists went out and bought a new van, and crashed it, with some deaths and injuries, when he walked to the rear of the moving vehicle after placing it on "auto pilot!" My understanding is that the difference between "cruise control" and "auto pilot" actually became a briefing topic in the "welcome aboard" package for new foreign students.

From Leukemia to the Texas Crud in El Paso

I became critically ill and my life was in danger in this instance. I was on active duty at Fort Bliss, Texas, and did not feel very good. I went to the Beaumont Army Hospital, and in a short period of time it was established that I was a very sick person. In fact, a couple of specialists were brought in to examine me (it was in the evening), and the possibilities ranged from leukemia to mononucleosis. It was made very clear to me that I was very sick. Additional blood was drawn and I was directed to return to my quarters, get in bed, and call the next morning for the results of the additional tests.

When I called the next morning, the doctor said I was okay, just had a case of the "Texas Crud" and that I would be fine in a day or so. I was scheduled to drive back to California that day, had Jake with me, and the doctor said that would be acceptable and that I was fit for the trip. I really felt horrible, but if the doctor said that I was okay, I guessed that I was okay.

It was a difficult trip back to Los Angeles. I felt terrible, and on several occasions actually had to stop and lie down alongside the highway.

When I got home, my entire body was vibrating and it was clear that something was very wrong. I called the inspector-instructor at the reserve unit, and he sent a driver to fetch me and take me to the Long Beach Naval Hospital.

I was rushed into the emergency room, where my symptoms included urinating blood. I was in sad shape. It turns out that I had advanced mononucleosis, that my spleen was the size of a football because my condition had not been caught in time, and the mono had developed into hepatitis!

I was put into isolation and spent two weeks in that hospital, and for the next year could still feel the effects of my illness and experienced very serious fatigue in the first couple of months. The naval medical personnel contacted the Beaumont Army Medical Center for a summary of my treatment, and were told there was no record of my having ever been there! I wrote a personal letter to the very nice Army physician who initially treated me, and who called in the specialists, but never received a reply.

Wing Vs. Division

This is as good a place as any to discuss my perception of being assigned to the Marine Air Wing versus the Marine Division (ground forces). I have always seen myself as a ground/infantry type of Marine, and have preferred to be assigned to "division" as opposed to the "wing." Without suggesting one is better than the other, there are big differences. Basically, the wing exists for one reason and that is to fly aircraft and other aviation related tasks. Almost without exception, the folks calling the shots in the wing are naval aviators (pilots) and those who are not pilots are, to some extent, in my judgment, second-class citizens. It was always subtle, but always a factor. I had some great experiences in my wing assignments, but always felt more comfortable when assigned to a Marine division (ground).

A "Smokey Bear" Campaign Hat for Captain Bushey

While assigned in Pasadena, I had the time available for a second period of summer active duty, and sought a two-week assignment in the Greater Washington, D.C. area. I reached out to a pal at the 4th Marine Air Wing Headquarters, retired Chief Warrant Officer Scotty Ernce. He couldn't find a suitable school or assignment for me, but I refused to take no for an answer, and asked him to keep looking.

Finally, he called and told me that I had just been assigned as the company commander of a two-week marksmanship instructor's course at the Weapons Training Battalion at the Marine Corps Base, Quantico, Virginia. I was not that thrilled, because it meant hours and hours of "snapping in," assuming and holding a number of convoluted body positions to facilitate accurate shooting posture, and I told him so. He responded that I should be careful of what I asked for, and to enjoy the course!

The course was two weeks of shooting and snapping in, as part of the requirements that led to graduation and designation as a primary marksmanship instructor (PMI). I was thrilled to be presented with the coveted "Smokey Bear" campaign hat that PMIs are authorized to wear when providing marksmanship instruction, but it remained on my wall as opposed to my head, as I never exercised the skills that I acquired during those two weeks at the Weapons Training Battalion. Overall, I did enjoy the training, and feel that I did well as the company commander.

The Missing Physical Examination

I did something, or failed to do something, in Pasadena, that did not set well with the inspector-instructor, Major Phil Norton. In the Marine Corps Reserve, captains could always find a paid billet, but sometimes it got a little tough (or so I thought at the time) for a major to find one.

It was not unusual for people to delay the mandatory physical examination that always preceded the formal promotion after the selection board met and announced a pending promotion, but I really stretched the issue.

For almost two years after having been selected for major, I failed to take the physical, and finally got a blast from Headquarters Marine Corps to take my physical or else (I don't know what "else" might have been, but it would not have been nice!) I was promoted to the rank of major just before transferring from Pasadena, and my failure to take the physical in a timelier manner was among the issues that Major Norton found troubling. Captain was a great rank, with those who held this rank often referred to as the "skipper," and it was somewhat of a sad day when I pinned on the gold oak leaves of a major.

Not Selected as the New Commanding Officer

Although there were no guarantees, there was an expectation at the time that I became the executive officer of 4th FAAD that I would also become the next commanding officer, but that was not to be. At that time, the next commanding officer was basically the person who was supported by the inspector-instructor, and the wing commander, who made the appointment, almost always honored that recommendation. While I believe that I did a good job and was the most worthy and deserving for the position, I did not have the support of the "old guard," the several staff non-commissioned and warrant officers who had spent just about their entire careers in Pasadena, and these folks embarked on an anti-Bushey lobbying effort with the inspector-instructor, that had an influence in me not getting that command. Other factors that influenced my non-selection, in my judgment, was my failure to take my promotion physical in a timely manner (not a big thing if that was the only issue), but primarily my perceived closeness to the previous troublesome inspector-instructor, Ron Arnold (likely the key factor). A subsequent return to the Pasadena Marine Corps Reserve Unit was not in the cards.

About six or seven years later, while wrapping up my tour as the commanding officer of 3D ANGLICO, I met the then-inspector-instructor of the 4th Forward Area Air Defense Battery in Pasadena at a social function. His name was Major Kim Stalnaker, and he seemed like a very solid and competent fellow. We chatted quite a bit and, knowing that I was wrapping up a successful command tour, he initiated a conversa-tion about me potentially returning to Pasadena and assuming command of 4th FAAD. I told him of my past with Pasadena and how I had not been selected previously, and my disdain over the good old boy network that existed there. He had exactly the same concerns, but pretty much assured me that any heartburn was long past, and encouraged me to apply. I did apply; my package went to the commanding officer of the Marine Air Control Group at Glencoe, Illinois, the higher headquarters where the selection, subject to ratification by the Wing commanding general, was really made.

Major Stalnaker called me, mad as hell, and said that another person was being selected, and the group commanding officer really did not give much of a reason. I called the group commanding officer myself, and got jacked around with no real answer other than he had someone in mind that he felt was a better selection. That someone turned out to be a pilot from the east coast who someone in the chain of command wanted to take good care of!

That type of nonsense occurred more than it should have. I was a tenured commander with the proper military occupational specialty who lived about twelve miles from the unit, but they selected someone who had never worked in the field who had to commute a couple of thousand miles for the reserve drill meetings! It was also a reflection of the preferential treatment often shown to pilots, over non-pilots, in the air wing, and one of the big reasons that I preferred the "ground side of the house." In hindsight, I am very fortunate not to have been selected, as it created other "fork in my road" that turned out much better.

Chapter Eighteen
MARINE AIR SUPPORT SQUADRON FOUR (MASS 4)

In March 1983 after five years in Pasadena, I transferred to Marine Air Support Squadron Four (MASS-4) at El Toro, and started the process to become a fully qualified air support control officer. Within the Police Department, at the time of my transfer to MASS-4, I was the commanding officer of the West Los Angeles Field Services (Patrol) Division. Shortly thereafter, I was promoted to the level of Captain II (and shortly thereafter again to Captain III) where I was triple-hatted as the Commanding Officer of Communications Division, the Project Manager of the Emergency Command, Control, and Communications Project, and as the LAPD representative (several trips each year) on Capitol Hill in Washington, D.C.

Rationale for Transferring to MCAS El Toro

It was clear that I was not going to get the top job in Pasadena, so I made application to join Marine Air Support Squadron Four (MASS-4), a subordinate unit of Marine Air Group Forty-Six (MAG-46) of the 4th Marine Air Wing (3rd MAW), at the Marine Corps Air Station at El Toro, California. I knew a bunch of the Marines there and was immediately accepted, which was a good thing because I was still smarting from the Pasadena rejection.

The mission of MASS-4 was to train Marines to use the equipment and exercise the skills to manage Marine aircraft during the conduct of combat operations, such as taking control of tactical aircraft and coordinating the hand-off to forward observers, getting helo-borne troops into and out of drop zones, managing and deploying aircraft on strip-alerts, and related tasks. I think I would rather have been with a division (ground) outfit, but this assignment was available and the wing had far more major billets than did the ground division.

My First Exercise with MASS-4

I am a reasonably quick study with an adequate degree of intelligence. Within a month of joining MASS-4, I found myself as the officer-in-charge of the MASS detachment in support of a combined arms exercise (CAX) at the Marine Air-Ground Combat Center, Twenty-Nine Palms, California. Within a day or so, I was functioning in the Direct Air Support Center (DASC) as the Senior Air Director (SAD), performing the critical job of coordinating the control of numerous actual aircraft in a very sensitive operation. I spent a good portion of my career as a Marine officer getting assignments because of a perception that I possessed skills that I really did not possess, and then doing whatever was necessary to acquire those skills. This exercise was a good example of that trait.

Walker Spy Scandal and Loss Of My MOS!

In the mid-1980s, there was a massive scandal where a Navy warrant officer and his seaman son, John and Michael Walker, had been stealing extremely sensitive classified material and selling it to the Soviets. These two, especially the father, were in sensitive communications-security assignments, and used their access to betray our nation. One of the fall-outs was stripping hundreds of Navy and Marine personnel of military occupational specialties in the intelligence field if the holder of that MOS was no longer working in an intelligence assignment. My primary MOS was 0202 – Intelligence Officer, but I had not worked in that field since my tenure in the 14th Counterintelligence Team. By this time I had been selected for promotion to lieutenant colonel, but had no MOS! This was not good. I needed a new military occupational specialty.

Weak Performance and a Lousy Fitness Report– OUCH!

Most of the folks who are familiar with my military career would have to acknowledge that, for the most part, I did a good and professional job. However, my two-week assignment as the officer-in-charge of a Tactical Air Operations Center (TacCenter), during a Combined Arms Exercise (CAX) was not all that great. I had not been trained in TAC center operations, and my lacks of skills were reflected in my performance. I think I got through the exercise okay, but okay was not good enough, and my mistakes were obvious. Of the seven majors assigned to the unit [squadron] to which I was attached, the other six were all permanent members and pretty much knew their jobs.

For the first time in my military career, and the last time, I received an evaluation that placed me at the bottom of my fellow officers. I was not happy about this, and fretted because I was unfairly assigned to a job that I did not know, and among a group of officers who knew and pretty much looked out for each other professionally. The bottom line is that my performance was not that great.

In the Marine Corps, officers receive a numerical evaluation and "7 of 7" was a real adverse professional "hit." Fortunately for me, the majority of my other fitness reports as both a company and field-grade officer were uniformly very high, and overshadowed this one lousy fitness report when I came up for promotion to both lieutenant colonel and full colonel.

Air Support Control School

The Air Support Control School, as part of the Communications Schools, at Twenty-Nine Palms developed a two-week course for Air Support Control officers. By the time this course came along, I had been in the air support control field, with MASS-4, for a couple of years. I took the course and pretty much sailed through it. I submitted my request to Headquarters, Marine Corps, and was assigned the primary MOS of 7208 – Air Support Control Officer. I would have preferred a non-aviation MOS, but my MOS never assisted or hindered me in any of my aspirations, and it really did not make any difference. Besides, when I made full colonel, I was given the new MOS of 9906 – unrestricted ground colonel!

Captain, That Hapens to be Your Driver!

The air support control "coyote" (subject matter advisor and exercise evaluator) at the Marine Air-Ground Combat Center at Twenty-Nine Palms, Tony Broome (pseudonym) was a real dipshit. He was a very hyper and immature individual, and difficult to work with. Technically he was very savvy, but in terms of the real world, how to deal with people, and leadership issues, he was very weak. He was prone to "flame out" at even minor discrepancies, and was actually a disruptive influence when he was monitoring activities in the Direct Air Control Center (DASC).

One very hot afternoon he outdid himself on looking foolish. A Marine was very inappropriately tampering with a rattlesnake on OP (Observation Post) Crampton: he quickly grabbed the tail of the snake and started spinning it around until the snake's head connected with a rock and the reptile was instantly killed.

Broome started yelling about the troublesome behavior of the Marine, and the fact that we are suppose to be protecting wildlife, and demanded to know the unit to which the Marine who killed the snake was assigned. The Marine sheepishly reminded Broome that he was his (Broome's) driver! Those of us who did not care for Broome got quite a kick of this situation.

The "Short Term" Relationship In El Centro

In the early 1980s, I was a member of Marine Air Support Squadron Four, a reserve unit out of the Marine Corps Air Station, El Toro. We were serving our two weeks of active duty training at the Naval Auxiliary Airfield, El Centro, California. A fellow officer and somewhat of a strange personality Roger Loomis (pseudonym), a Mustang (former enlisted), who never stopped acting like a lance corporal, was among the other members of the Squadron taking part in the training.

After hours, Roger spent a lot of time at the Officers Club. About mid-way through the two weeks, he was trying his best to make time with a gal who was also spending a lot of time at the "O" Club. He was very persistent, and she finally told him straight out that she was not interested in a short term relationship, to which he replied: "Hey, I will be here until Friday!"

Weenie Waver Waves at the Wrong People

During one of my many trips to the Marine Corps Base at Quantico, Virginia, to attend a professional development school, I was on a bus full of cops, who were also Marine Corps Reservists. We were all students at the FBI-USMC Law Enforcement Course, conducted at the FBI Academy, which was located on the base. We were en-route to the Army's Aberdeen Proving Grounds for a day of orientation with various automatic weapons.

While driving north on Interstate 95, a convertible pulled alongside the bus and the driver, a lone male, was smiling at all of us as he masturbated! We all alternated between red-hot anger and uncontrollable laughter, as there was nothing we could do. We could not even get a license number because of the position of the car in relation to the bus. After a few minutes, he veered off and disappeared. I suspect he would really have been pleased had he known that he was exposing himself to several dozen cops.

Shooting at the White House

In March of 1984, I was one of about twenty reserve Marines, all of who were civilian peace officers, who were on active duty at Headquarters, Marine Corps, as part of a group to study and make recommendations pertaining to the then-fairly recent bombing at the

Marine Barracks in Lebanon. In fact, the head of my task team was Lieutenant Colonel Oliver North, who later gained much fame as part of a White House scandal. Jake accompanied me on this trip.

One evening, Jake badgered me into taking him for a walk around the White House perimeter, and we ended up as the two witnesses to the unsuccessful efforts of a deranged man to jump the fence and assassinate then-President Ronald Reagan. He had a shotgun under his coat, and pulled it out when the uniformed Secret Service officers, who had been watching him, chose to approach him. They shot him in the arm, and took him into custody. Jake and I became real celebrities for a day or so, and Jake was eventually the key witness in the trial held several months later in Washington. This incident resulted in us meeting key uniformed Secret Service personnel, and enjoying a number of nice after-hours visits to the White House, which paid off during my many LAPD trips to Washington during my ultimately successful lobbying efforts for additional radio channels for public safety.

A Great Landing of an F-4 Phantom – Well, Almost

On a Saturday morning while I was at my desk at MASS-4, chaos started to reign, and a bunch of sirens were activated. It seems that an F-4 was lined up for a perfect landing, descended with maximum proficiency and performance, and flared perfectly; unfortunately, the pilot forgot to lower the landing gear (wheels!) I was among the "looky-loos" who descended on-site, which was a damaged plane, flat on the ground, with weeds embedded on just about all ground-level surfaces.

The pilot and the bombardier-navigator (also known as the radar intercept officer – RIO) had some pretty long faces, and with good justification; they knew their flying days were immediately over and that their time in the Marine Corps was not going to be much longer. That poor plane remained in the headquarters hanger of MAG-46 (Marine Air Group), which was the higher headquarters to all the reserve squadrons, including mine, for several months, with the weeds still sticking out of the front apertures. It was in the process of being phased out as the F-18s were starting to trickle in to the reserves, and it was ultimately scrapped rather than being repaired.

I did not run into the pilot or the RIO after that, but knew that their flying days were over, and that whatever was left in their USMC careers was sure to be menial until they were released from active duty. Certainly, there was an investigation and a subsequent Board of Inquiry, but there is not much of a defense for failure to lower the landing gear on a million dollar airplane.

Female Staff Sergeant – Fraternization or Restraint?

At the time that I held the rank of major, during my tour in MASS 4, I met and struck up a very nice platonic relationship with a full-time ("regular") female staff sergeant. It was clear to both of us that we would like to have a relationship that went beyond platonic. However the Marine Corps not only frowned on fraternization between officers and enlisted personnel, but also actually court-martialed some officers and drummed them out of the Marine Corps for nothing other than having had a romantic relationship with a female enlisted Marine.
Barbara, (the female staff sergeant), went out of her way to assure me that she had the ability to be very discreet, and that she was anxious for her and I to become romantically involved. This was tough for me because I was single and not seeing anyone at that particular time, and Barbara had no shortage of qualities that I found to be attractive. She was a photo-journalist in the base public affairs office, and there was no way that we would even be in the same chain of command, but even being on separate continents would not have been acceptable as long as she was an enlisted Marine.

In the end, however, restraint won out over passion and our relationship did not go beyond the platonic stage. Barbara was a nice gal with a lot to offer, but I had too much to lose by crossing that forbidden line. I continue to remain strong in my belief that the Marine Corps anti-fraternization policy is a bit too strict, and should not apply in some situations involving different commands when no work-place conflict is involved. I hate to sound like a romantic, and I do clearly recognize that there is most often more lust than love involved in fraternization, however there are times when the chemistry between two persons is so strong that they are meant to be together, and for that reason I believe some flexibility on the issue is appropriate.

As I reflect on the above situation, I feel very sorry for Barbara and other women in the same position. For me, it was just a potential opportunity that never came to fruition. For Barbara, it was a continuing saga of heartache and disappointments. Her world was a virtual whopper pond of men, many of whom were single, but a good portion of those who were of intellectual and social interest were off-limits because they were commissioned and she was enlisted. Although very smart, well-educated, and with previous journalism experience before entering the military, she fell short of a baccalaureate degree needed for commissioning, and was not selected for a warrant officer program. I suspect she left the Corps, as such would have been understandable.

The End of My Tour at MASS-4

My tour in MASS-4 was drawing to an end. Again, I was the heir apparent to be the new commanding officer when fate again intervened. In reorganization, it was decided that MASS-4 would be downgraded from squadron to detachment status. This was bad for me personally, because a squadron is commanded by a lieutenant colonel (which I was about to be) and a major commands a detachment, which is what the unit was about to be downgraded to. It was clear that I was on the verge of being promoted out of a job, and certainly would not be the next commanding officer. Because of the 3D ANGLICO selection several months later, this redesignation was a blessing in disguise for me, as I would not have competed for 3D ANGLICO if I had gotten the MASS-4 commanding officer's position.

Chapter Nineteen
MOBILIZATION TRAINING UNIT CA-49

In October 1988, after approximately five years in MASS 4, I transferred to the Mobilization Training Unit CA-49. This was truly a "holding pattern" until something better came along.

My First (and *ONLY*) Unpaid Billet

Mobilization Training Units (MTUs) are somewhat of an organizational bone yard for senior officers who cannot find a paid billet, or who for whatever reason(s) chose not to serve in the more demanding paid billet status. These are unpaid assignments where points are awarded for weekend drill participation, but that is it. Realistically, very little is expected other than showing up, allegedly participating in some continuing military education, and sometimes doing minor projects.

A few of the folks in this outfit, which was commanded by a civilian airline pilot, Colonel "Birdie" Bertrand, volunteered in helping to develop the new command museum at El Toro. I needed a holding pattern until something else came along, and "Birdie" joined me to this MTU. For the several months that I was there, I spent most of my time back at MASS-4 in a quasi-command position (but in unpaid status), as the imminent transition from squadron to detachment status had not yet occurred.

Screwed Out of Attending the Royal War College

The "Good Old Boy Pilot's Club" struck again, and I am still pissed about being screwed out of something I worked hard to obtain. While still in paid status as a member of MASS-4, I competed successfully and was selected to attend the two-week military exchange course of the British Royal War College in Poole, England. While in MASS-4, my higher headquarters was the 4th Marine Aircraft Wing in New Orleans, where virtually all of the key staff members were pilots. When I fell into unpaid status, a couple of those bastards decided that one of them should take my place at the Royal War College, and saw my change to unpaid drill status as the opportunity to strike.

The G-3 (Operations & Training) at the Wing in New Orleans notified me that they would not pay to send me to England, so they cancelled my attendance for the course! What he did not say is that it would have been perfectly acceptable to permit me to attend, that I was the one who competed and was selected by Headquarters Marine Corps (CMC) based on my superb performance in the Wing, that it was favoritism and not funding driving their actions, and that "Wing" had advised CMC that I was no longer available, thus providing another name as a substitute, (obviously one of the pilot bubbas at Wing Headquarters). Interestingly, my temporary unpaid assignment was at El Toro Air Station and I was still in support of the Wing!! While I had and have a great many USMC aviator pals, and while there are no shortage of unique personalities on the ground side of the Marine Corps either, this type of stupid pilot favoritism was not uncommon at the higher levels in Marine Corps aviation.

Chapter Twenty
3D AIR-NAVAL GUNFIRE LIAISON COMPANY (3D ANGLICO)

In July 1989, after several months in the Mobilization Training Unit at El Toro, I assumed command of 3D ANGLICO. Since my previous tour in this unit, it had relocated to a nice new reserve center at the Long Beach Naval Station. This unit is absolutely one of the most coveted commands in the Marine Corps Reserve, and ranked right alongside, and maybe a cut above, being assigned as a battalion commander.

The two organizational companies in the Marine Corps, reserve and regular that are commanded by a lieutenant colonel are ANGLICO and Force Reconnaissance. The key mission is to provide Marine forward observers to either the U.S. Army or allied military forces to coordinate the acquisition of Naval Gunfire or Marine Close Air Support. Most of the key operation billets, including the entire command staff, were airborne designated (parachutist). There was no job in the Marine Corps that I would rather have had than to command 3D ANGLICO, and having held that position remains the highlight of my Marine Corps career. At the time, within the police department, I was a captain III and assigned as the commanding officer of the Wilshire Area. About half way through my two-year ANGLICO command tour, I was reassigned by the LAPD and became the commanding officer of the Northeast Area.

The Command Officer Interview For 3D ANGLICO

The command tour of then-Lieutenant Colonel Mike Kromm was drawing to a close and the process to select a new commanding officer, from well over a dozen "high-speed, low-drag" lieutenant colonels was under way. This process consisted of the outgoing commanding officer and the inspector-instructor, Joe Scott, interviewing all the candidates and making a recommendation to the commanding general of the 4th Marine Division, Major General Walter Boomer. The process started out as a sham, and it rapidly became clear that they had a favorite candidate and were not taking the other applicants seriously.

When I appeared as scheduled for my interview with Kromm and Scott, they were not there. The first sergeant advised that they were en-route back from Camp Pendleton, were running late, and asked that I await their return for my interview. A few minutes later, another applicant, with whom I was acquainted, also showed up for his interview, and he was asked to wait also.

After about an hour, Kromm and Scott showed up and announced that they were going to interview the two of us together! Those two did all the talking and painted a dismal picture of the demands on the commanding officer, pretty much attempting to downplay the position and discouraging our interest. Finally, Joe Scott said that the interview was over and also said: "I will be honest with both of you, we will just send all the names to division and do not know how the selection will be made!"

I tore, diplomatically but with no room for misunderstanding, into both Kromm and Scott and told them they were not being honest, that they knew exactly how the process worked, that they obviously had a favorite candidate in mind, that the process was a sham, that they were letting down "the Boomer" (implying that I had some relationship with the commanding general – which I did not), and that the two of them should be ashamed of themselves for not performing their duties in a professional and ethical manner. I told them that I had spent hours preparing for the interview and was conversant on every critical issue facing the unit, but that none of those issues was even mentioned.

I stood, dropped my resume in front of them, and told them to give me a call if either of them decided to get serious about their responsibilities! Kromm tried to explain that the typical interview was not really necessary because they had our resumes, and I reminded him that as a businessman, (insurance as I recall), he would not have hired an office worker without more of an interview than occurred in this instance. I then walked out.

I told a friend of mine, Chief Warrant Officer Scotty Ernce, at division headquarters, what had occurred, and I believe that he told General Boomer what happened. I think that this probably caused the commanding general to pay close attention to the process.

The general did not know me, but if this was the case it certainly did me no harm, and made the process a cleaner one. I know that my stock was good with Scotty and suspect that his stock was good with General Boomer, and that may well have been a factor that influenced my ultimate selection.

The next day I got a call from Joe Scott and was invited back for an interview with him. I was truly prepared for the interview, and encouraged him to invite his entire staff to listen to my thoughts and presentation – I could feel that it went very well. Then Kromm and I met downtown for a prolonged lunch, and again I felt good that it went well.

A month or so later, while attending the Command & Staff College at Quantico, I was notified that I had been selected as the new commanding officer of 3D ANGLICO! I was walking on water and was the envy of most of the other students for having been selected for one of the most coveted commands in the Marine Corps Reserve.

Joe Scott and I went on to be great friends, but I never asked, and he never volunteered the name of the person that he and Kromm were pushing for the position. I think it might have been Kromm's executive officer, a Marine pilot with silver jump wings from NROTC, but who declined my strong suggestion, when I became the commanding officer, that he return to active jump status. I replaced him with Wes May as my executive officer. The pilot, whose name escapes me, was gracious in leaving.

Lieutenant Colonel Bushey Featured in *Leatherneck* Magazine

For some unknown reason, the staff of the *Leatherneck* Magazine selected me as a Marine Corps success story. Someone thought that going from a private and high school dropout to a lieutenant colonel commanding 3D ANGLICO was worth writing about. I was flattered to be selected for this honor, and pleased at the article. It appeared in the March 1990 edition. As a humorous footnote, the staff writer wanted to include a photo of my kids but they were angry, (I do not recall what about), when I brought them together for the photos; Zak was fine but because of the scowl on the faces of Jake and Stacy, the photo could not be used!

The Commanding Officer's Crash Landing at Camp Pendleton

I had not been active as a parachutist since my first tour in ANGLICO, which ended eleven years prior. I was rusty in this critical area. In preparation for my first jump as the commanding officer, Gunnery Sergeants Frank Brown and Scotty Anderson came to my home in Azusa, brought main and reserve parachutes, suited me up, and had me do a bunch of parachute landing falls (PLFs) off the back of a pick-up truck onto my lawn.

After a month or two as the commanding officer, we had a C-141 jump over the Tank Park drop zone (DZ) at Camp Pendleton. As per the custom, I was the first jumper out of the aircraft, loved the jump and descent, but really crashed and burned when landing! I did not do a very good PLF (parachute landing fall) and landed wrong and hit hard. I managed to hobble for the final formation, but had trouble walking for a few days.

I finally healed, or so I thought, but now, in my mid-60s, I have a few aches and pains and know that this poor landing did some damage that was masked by youth and fitness. I had an MRI done on my back and hips a couple of years ago, and several injuries are apparent. Just one of those things that goes with an active lifestyle, and I would not trade my experiences for anything. I did not seek medical attention at the time for fear that it would jeopardize my command assignment.

Most of the men whom I know and served with are like old rodeo riders. We have a few aches and pains, decreased mobility, are hurting at times, but smile at the thought of the incidents that caused these injuries. These problems are likely to get worse as I continue to age, but that is just the way things are. I will hobble with pride!

Called Out of the Field -Near Fatal Shooting of a Police Officer

In 1990, during the wee small hours of a remote weekend field exercise at Camp Pendleton, a military police officer was able to track me down and deliver a message that I was to call the watch commander of the Los Angeles Police Department Northeast Area, which I commanded as my civilian occupation. It turned out that a suspect who, not realizing that his intended female victim was an armed off-duty police officer, tried to carjack her pick-up truck had shot one of my officers, Stacy Lim. She managed to shoot and kill the suspect, but only after he shot her point-blank in the chest with a high-powered handgun. I responded immediately to the Henry Mayo Hospital in Newhall and, with my wife, sat with Stacy's family during the major surgery that was underway in a desperate attempt to save her life.

As the sun came up, the surgeon advised us that all that could be done had been done, and it was now in "God's hands." Cathy and I went home but almost immediately got a call from the hospital that serious internal bleeding had started and perhaps we desired to be with the family as she "slipped away." We rushed back to the hospital and upon arrival were told that "there had been a miracle," and that the internal bleeding had stopped. That wonderful young woman experienced a full recovery and to this day remains an active police officer and vigorous athlete. Miracles do happen.

Jumping into an Inkwell!

Night parachute operations are inherently dangerous, but reflect very necessary training for Marine parachutists. In combat situations, the likelihood of being able to pick and choose the drop zone location and time of the jump is non-existent. One of the more memorable night jumps was into the "Tank Park" drop zone at Camp Pendleton. It was completely dark, not much moonlight, but with some ambient light from the city of Oceanside approximately ten miles to the south.

We were jumping from a C-130 Hercules four engine transport. To reduce the likelihood of colliding with another jumper, we all had chemical glow sticks attached to our parachute harnesses. As the commanding officer, I was the first person out of the aircraft, and standing on the lowered ramp with all the noise and wind, and looking down into what I thought of as an inkwell, was not among the more enjoyable things that I have done.

While waiting for the word to "go" I asked myself "What the f—k am I doing this for, when I could be sitting at home in my easy chair?" Then another thought occurred to me: What a privilege that I am still in the arena, being a United States Marine, doing exciting things, while all of my childhood buddies were sitting in their easy chairs, drinking beer, and getting fat! The final thought was very motivating and went I got the word to "go" I had a big smile on my face.

Approaching the ground in a parachute when it is dark is truly an exciting experience! While you can get some idea of when you are about to hit the ground by watching the horizon, you usually have no idea as to what you are about to land on until it happens, hopefully an open area but not always. My landing in this operation was fine, but three of my men were seriously injured during the landing, the most serious being Major Fritz Bystrum, a great fellow and an attorney in Los Angeles when not a Marine. All three were hospitalized, with Fritz requiring several surgeries due to a severe leg injury.

Preparing Men for Combat

I took my job very seriously because of the importance of the mission, and the likelihood that there may not have been much time for training in the event of mobilization for an actual real-world deployment. This has always been a driving force with me, and has not always served me well, such as in Pasadena where it sometimes appeared that the primary consideration was keeping people, even those with questionable skills, alive in the USMCR. I truly like, covet, and respect the social and fraternal side of the Marine Corps, but the primary issue must be readiness to be immediately deployed for combat operations. Too many people fail to have this as a priority.

In August of 1990, my executive officer, Lieutenant Colonel Wes May and his family were vacationing with my family, at our home in Big Bear. On a Saturday morning, August 5, a news bulletin announced that Iraqi Forces had just invaded Kuwait. Wes and I looked at each other with special recognition, as we were aware that such an incident involving these counties was among the situations that would trigger the activation of 3D ANGLICO.

If possible to do so, we further enhanced our training and readiness activities. We knew that we would be activated; we just did not know when the activation would occur.

Liaison Officer to the 5th Division – Japanese Self-Defense Force

One brigade platoon was activated and deployed to Camp Lejeune in North Carolina, and the rest of 3D ANGLICO, with me at the helm, were awaiting our orders as well. It was obvious that allied forces would eventually invade Kuwait and chase the Iraqis back into Iraq, but not until the troop build-up was complete. It was not complete at the time that 3D ANGLICO was tasked with providing a small detachment to the Third Marine Expeditionary Force (III MEF) to support a joint US-Japanese exercise, Yama Sakura, at Camp Chotise on the island of Hokkaido in Japan. I felt it would be a fun trip and that as a lieutenant colonel I would be able to just kick back and enjoy the trip – boy, was I wrong!

We first went to Okinawa and joined the III MEF Marines who were also assigned to the exercise, and then flew in a C-130 to Camp Chotose. When the two staffs, American and Japanese, met for a social function, with plenty of sake, before the exercise began, the Japanese commander made it very clear that he expected that the Marine staff officer assigned to his staff as liaison officer be among the best, brightest, and most knowledgeable members of the III MEF staff. As I was trying to speculate as who this super person would be, Major General Henry "Hank" Stackpole, the commanding general of III MEF, announced that they had carefully selected such a person and that he was Lieutenant Colonel Bushey. I spent the next week or so with the Japanese and did a decent job; again, I got in there and did my best and things went well.

This trip afforded me the opportunity to spend a few days on Okinawa, where I had not been since I was a lance corporal in 1964! I took a bunch of walks down memory lanes and truly enjoyed the visit. I went to my old squad bay, workspaces, recreational areas, mess halls, and the grinder where I was standing when told of President Kennedy's assassination.

For awhile, it appeared that 3D ANGLICO was going to be attached to III MEF for a one year tour, and that I would be designated as the executive officer of the 3rd Surveillance, Reconnaissance, and Intelligence Group (SRIG). When I visited the commanding officer of 3rd SRIG, I went into the same building where I used to buff the floors when the facility was the headquarters of the 9th Marine Amphibious Force! That assignment, which for some complicated reasons would have been very desirable, did not come to pass. I am so grateful that I had the opportunity to visit a location that was so prominent in my teenage years.

Note: There is quite a story involving General Stackpole. When he was a captain in Vietnam, he was gravely wounded and thought to be dead. As personnel, including a Navy chaplain, were doing triage and separating the wounded from the deceased Marines, the chaplain thought he detected a slight sign of life in Captain Hank Stackpole's body. Stackpole was removed from the deceased holding area and given immediate medical attention. Obviously, he survived and went on to a distinguished career, ultimately retiring as a lieutenant general. The Navy chaplain who detected the signs of life and who is responsible for Stackpole's life is Commander (now retired) Victor Krulak, Jr., oldest son of retired Lieutenant General Victor "Brute" Krulak, USMC, one of the true legends of the Marine Corps. Chaplain Krulak saved a good man and a great Marine leader, and someone who was certainly good to me.

"Make Sure There is a *Charlie* Available for the Old Man!"

During my first tour in 3D ANGLICO, we used the standard T-10 parachute. It had no steering capability other than climbing the risers while descending in an attempt, usually unsuccessful, to cause the chute to descend in a desired direction. When I returned to 3D ANGLICO, we had the new and improved parachute, the MC1-1 "Bravo," which was essentially a T-10 that was modified to permit some control by the installation of two toggles that the jumper could pull to partially collapse portions of the canopy, in order to control the downward drift. Clearly, the "Bravo" was a real improvement over the T-10. However, like the T-10, the typical decent speed of the "Bravo" was 16 to 22 feet per second, which means you screamed in pretty fast.

While at 3D ANGLICO, we took delivery of several MC1-1 "Charlies," which, because the material in the canopy was woven more closely together, it had a much slower typical speed of 8 to 12 feet per second. With my aging body being beaten pretty badly and regularly with hard landings, I fell in love with the relatively soft landings provided for when using the new 'chutes. Towards the end of my tour, the parachute riggers made sure that there was always a "Charlie" available for the "old man" (me)!

"I Would Rather Have a Mannequin than Captain Webb"

Being called to active duty was not a matter of "if," but just a matter of "when." While some people were anxiously anticipating the call-up, others were not necessarily enthusiastic, but just about everyone realized it was necessary and that is why we served in the Marine Corps Reserve. The one exception was Captain Jeff Webb (pseudonym), a pilot (C-130) who joined the unit about six months prior.

Captain Webb was in a very critical close air support (CAS) position, and had just completed a very coveted and hard to get assignment to the Tactical Air Support Party (TACP) course at Coronado, a school that he literally begged me to permit him to attend over other applicants. As we were going through mobilization preparation, Captain Webb advised me that he desired to "go Class 3" (inactive reserve) because his wife and his employer did not want him to mobilize!

I had a long and fatherly conversation with Captain Webb about both personal and professional issues, about the need the unit had for the critical skills that he possessed, and about his obligation to Corps and County; we invested a great deal in him and now it was time to reap the needs of that investment, and that his absence would weaken the unit's combat readiness. My words, and those of his platoon commander, fell on deaf ears and he transferred to the inactive reserve.

His platoon commander created a scathing special fitness report that referred to him in very unflattering terms, and what the platoon commander said was charitable compared to what I added in my endorsement. Captain Webb was very unhappy with his adverse fitness report and requested mast (tantamount to a military equivalent of a civilian grievance). The reviewing officer, a colonel on the staff of the 4th Marine Division in New Orleans, placed his endorsement on the fitness report, and in referring to Captain Webb, made the comment, "I would rather have a mannequin attached to my unit than Captain Webb." That worthless person actually felt, and told me so, that he just needed to take a few months off, but would return to the active reserves after the Gulf War was over! When he walked out of my office that was the last time he wore the uniform of a United States Marine.

Called Up for the First Gulf War

In early December of 1990, one brigade platoon, (slightly less than one-third of 3D ANGLICO), was activated for the Gulf War, and the rest of us knew that it was just a matter of time before the entire unit was activated. Unfortunately, in my judgment, we were not activated as soon as we should have been.

I made several trips to New Orleans (Division Headquarters) for consultations in preparation for activation, but it was not happening.

I finally lobbied hard with our commanding general, Major General Cooper, (Boomer had pinned on his third star and was now the commanding general of I MEF in the Southwest Asia theater, commanding all Marine ground forces in preparation for combat operations), and my direct boss, the G-3, Colonel Sexton, to get us activated. It worked, but we were not activated until the third day of the four-day war!

As we arrived at Camp Pendleton, hostilities ceased. My advanced party, the 2nd Brigade Platoon that had been activated, did a great job and destroyed 230 Iraqi vehicles at a place called Al Wafra, for which I as their commanding officer also received accolades. I was green with envy at my troops who made it into combat, and wish the entire unit could have been engaged as well. My disappointment, and that of just about all of my men who did not get into combat, was very strong.

The War of Retention on Active Duty!

Now I had a new battle on my hands: keeping my troops on active duty for at least ninety days so as to ensure their eligibility for a whole array of veteran's benefits. Within a week or so of the end of the ground war in Kuwait/Iraq, the efforts got underway to start releasing reserves back to civilian life. This was really a pain, because a number of my folks made some pretty big sacrifices for activation (relinquished child custody, worked with employers for long-term replacements, etc.), and now it looked like a short evolution. While some of my people were anxious to return to civilian life, most of them preferred to stay on active duty for a while and maybe even deploy as part of the occupation. Also, General Stackpole's desire for us to serve for a year on Okinawa was still potentially viable at that point.

Camp Pendleton – Del Mar Area

As long as we were going to be at Camp Pendleton for a few months, I decided to see how much critical training, and critical administrative requirements, I could achieve, and had to have set some type of a record for what one unit could accomplish in three months! I have always been pretty savvy in knowing the system, and in getting things done in spite of the bureaucracy, and those skills really paid off in this endeavor.

The following were accomplished in the ninety-six days we were on active duty: Every Marine receive the annual physical, forty-nine Marines completed jump school, approximately two dozen additional Marines obtained military drivers licenses, approximately two dozen of my communications personnel obtained technician level amateur radio licenses (I brought in outside volunteer instructors), Landing Force Training Command – Pacific (Coronado) developed and provided to several dozen of the Marines a one week course on frequency propagation and the construction of field expedient high frequency radio antennas, all Marines completed the yearly marksmanship qualification with their designated weapon, all basic parachutist made the necessary additional jumps and received the Navy-Marine Corps Parachutist Badge, all Marines who required dental work had that work performed, every service record book (enlisted) and qualifications jacket (officer) was audited and updated, a detachment completed the Mountain Warfare training Course at Bridgeport (California), and a great deal of additional individual training was accomplished.

All of these activities placed the unit in a superb position, and essentially cleared the decks of those issues that interfere with training for at least the next twelve to eighteen months. These accomplishments, along with the superb combat performance of my advanced party, contributed to my being awarded the Meritorious Service Medal, receiving a phenomenal fitness report from Lieutenant General Boomer, and no doubt contributed to my selection to full colonel several months later.

The "Phantom Pooper!"

If I live to be 100, I will never understand why some people (fortunately very few) get satisfaction from surreptitiously defecating in a conspicuous location, obviously with the intent to gross out other people. I have encountered this syndrome another time or two during my Marine Corps career. In this instance, the suspect deposited a big pile of fecal matter in the middle of the floor in the barrack's head (large common bathroom).

Sergeant Major Trumbich got to the bottom of the matter and established conclusively, but not legally, that the suspect was a well-respected master sergeant. He always had an odd side, but this was quite a surprise. He had applied for the warrant officer program, and I was in the process of creating an enthusiastic endorsement at the time of this incident; obviously, I did not provide the endorsement. He knew that we knew, but couldn't prove it to a legal standard. He also knew that I withdrew the endorsement, and why. It was suggested that he seek counseling, but he denied the incident, although he did not protest very strongly. There were no overt consequences, but he was watched pretty closely after this. He was a pretty profane and earthly fellow who probably did not see this as seriously as others. He remained in the unit after my command tour was over, and eventually retired from the Marine Corps Reserve.

Police Motorcycle in the Garage

 *No clank*

Gunnery Sergeant William "Willie" Sampson was among the number of Los Angeles Police officers who served under me as reservists in 3D ANGLICO. He was a Valley Traffic Division motorcycle officer whose seniority resulted in him having been issued a brand new motorcycle not long before he was activated for the Gulf War. When he told me he would have the exact same motorcycle when he returned to the Department, I commented that it would have about a year of additional mileage on it because it would have been reassigned to another "motor" officer in his absence, but he confidently replied that would not be the case. When I asked incredulously if the Department would just put it in storage for him, he cryptically told me that he never turned it in and that it was sitting in his garage at home! He explained that this was done with the tacit approval of his supervisors! As a long-time LAPD command officer, I knew this was contrary to every rule, law and practice of the LAPD and I was both shocked and amused. I just kept Bill's secret to myself and chuckled every time I thought about the issue.

Dusty Detective Car at the Ranges of Camp Pendleton

On a couple of occasions, while on remote ranges back in the hills of Camp Pendleton, I noticed what appeared to be an unmarked police vehicle, with Minnesota license plates, driving on the dirt roads. It was dirty and dusty with much caked mud in the fender wells. It had several antennas, including a big whip antenna on the rear, and suppressed emergency lights. Turns out that it was the duty vehicle of a Minnesota police detective, and when called to active duty he drove his police car to Camp Pendleton, and used it during the mobilization! Unbelievable!

The "Not So Great" Imposter

Captain Chad Wickham (pseudonym) was one of my very best performers and hard workers, and someone that I often called upon for tasks that were particularly difficult or complex. Not only was his performance superb, but his status as a former enlisted Marine ("Mustang"), and someone who was both wounded in action and decorated for bravery during the bombing of the Marine Barracks in Beirut (Lebanon) in 1983, weighed heavily in my favorable impression of him. As it turned out, he was a fraud! While his performance was legitimately superb and he was a "Mustang," he never served in Beirut, let alone having been wounded or decorated for bravery. As an investigation established, while in The Basic School (TBS) as a new lieutenant, he somehow had the meritorious record of another new lieutenant's placed in his Officer's Qualification Jacket (OQR).

Chad was brought down by too much libido and too many women who experienced that libido. He had a never-ending string of romantic encounters and just about all of them ended, as we later learned, with clear betrayal on his part. Unfortunately for him, one of his girlfriends, Michelle LaBelle (pseudonym), relished the opportunity to inflict pain as part of her revenge for his infidelity.

While at Camp Del Mar, Chad was thrilled that Michelle had invited him to move into her condo with him in nearby San Diego, not realizing that she had discovered that he was also involved with a couple of other women and that "moving day" would be a real bitch. After loading all of his possessions into her larger vehicle, the pair started driving south on Highway 101, with him behind her in his small car. Then the revenge started; she started throwing all of his prized possessions out the window of her car as they were doing 65 or so miles per hour down the crowded freeway! He watched his SCUBA tanks bounce across the median, his USMC engraved sword mangled by numerous vehicles, his dress blue uniform get caught in the tires of a big truck, etc., etc. etc.! The only thing she didn't throw out was something that she had sneaked out of his quarters: his "little black book!"

Michelle wasn't satisfied with ruining his possessions; she decided to ruin his life as well, but didn't realize just how successful she would be. *She called every woman listed in that book and invited them to a revenge meeting!* Because he lived in Orange County and all of his failed liaisons (there were no successful ones!) were in Southern California, and because he had created some much ill will with so many women, the meeting was apparently well attended.

When these gals started comparing notes, his life of lies started crumbling. Included among the issues that emerged were the falsification of military records, the covert sale of a Corvette that he reported stolen and had received an insurance settlement for, that he was never in Beirut or wounded, that he wore military decorations that he was not entitled to, and that his civilian resume included claims of having been a Marine F-18 pilot.

While others and myself knew of the situation on the freeway, we just assumed that Michelle was a scorned lover with a vicious streak, and pretty much felt sorry for Chad. When 3D ANGLICO was released from active duty, I permitted Chad to remain on active duty based upon the request of another colonel, Mike Brock, who wanted him to assist in a Department of Defense anti-drug interdiction mission.

Shortly thereafter, Michelle put together a massive document, in the form of a military charge sheet, outlining all of the information that emerged from the VWS (Vindictive Women's Summit) and faxed it to my colonel buddy. She then went personally to the colonel's command (1st Surveillance, Reconnaissance, and Intelligence Group) and demanded to see Colonel Brock, and became very irate when a clerk inquired as to the purpose of the visit.

She stormed through the entire building, yelling and screaming, and with a growing group of curious Marines following her, stormed into Mike's office, and then collapsed unconscious (drama-related fainting). As the paramedics were treating that unique woman, Mike called me (I was back in my LAPD office) with a blow-by-blow description of all the aforementioned drama.

Subsequent to an investigation, an administrative separation board was convened at 4th Marine Division headquarters in New Orleans, to determine Chad's suitability for continued service in the Marine Corps. He was denied travel pay to attend his own separations board, which was a bit of a hint that the Marine Corps wanted no part of this phony. Interestingly, he later applied for a position with the City of Los Angeles, and I was contacted as part of a background investigation. His resume was full of lies, including the F-18 pilot experience. This situation had to be an indication of an illness. Chad was truly a very capable and talented man, and could have been very successful in the Marine Corps without having to lie about anything. About his relationship with women; now that's another issue!

The Commanding Officer's Rear-View Mirror!

Subsequent to the Gulf War, 3D ANGLICO was given a place of special prominence in the annual Torrance Armed Forces Parade. However there was a problem, at least for me. The formation configuration required by the parade officials was one massive platoon as opposed to several platoons in line. That meant we had to have something like fifteen men across and twenty-five men deep. The commanding officer was to be centered in front of his command, about fifteen feet in front of the formation. The company gunnery sergeant was to be off to the side and calling cadence, but there was no way that I would be able to hear him. The likelihood of me looking stupid and being out of step was certain. However, I had an idea; develop a rear-view mirror for my helmet so that I could see my men and stay in step with them. I bought a dental mirror, painted it Marine green, and attached it to my helmet. It worked like a charm and I remained in step during the entire parade. I still have my "rear view mirror" and occasionally glance at it with funny fond memories.

Soviet Anti-Aircraft Gun Captured By 3D ANGLICO

I will never cease to be proud and honored by the outstanding performance of the men in my advanced party during the liberation of Kuwait. My troops really bloodied Suddam Hussein's nose by destroying approximately 230 of his armored vehicles. These outstanding Marines were led by one of my outstanding field grade officers, Major Bob Schonwetter. When the 56-hour war was over, Bob decided to bring home a Soviet anti-aircraft gun that his men had "neutralized" and seized. To those who know much about the military, bringing something like this back was a very difficult thing to do, but Bob managed to pull it off. Upon release from active duty, the unit marched in the Torrance Armed Forces Day Parade, and that captured gun was behind us on a trailer! It was then mounted in concrete outside the Reserve Center, then located on the Long Beach Naval Station. As part of base closures, that base no longer exists as a military reservation. That Anti-Aircraft gun captured by my men is now on permanent display in the courtyard outside the Command Museum at the Marine Corps Recruit Depot, San Diego. Some fifty-plus years ago, then Private Keith Bushey could not have imagined that he was standing at almost the exact location where the weapon's system captured by Colonel Bushey's troops would someday be displayed.

Accolades for 3D ANGLICO and Lieutenant Colonel Bushey

I consider myself to be very fortunate to have had such a successful command tour as commanding officer of the one of the Marine Corp's most elite, challenging, and important commands. From the day I took over until the day I turned over the command to Wes May, it was great! We accomplished so much, went so many places, had such rewarding experiences, and when called to active duty did a superb job. The roughly one-third of the unit who saw combat, my advanced party, distinguished themselves and destroyed approximately 230 Iraqi vehicles (and a bunch of Iraqis!) Like every command experience, it was the men who worked for me that made it all happen, but as the person at the helm I ended my command tour with many accolades, and was awarded the Meritorious Service Medal.

Surprise Award to Marine at West Los Angeles Roll Call

Staff Sergeant R. J. Cottle was among the Los Angeles police officers that were under my command at 3D ANGLICO. He was a great Marine and a great cop who was awarded the Navy Achievement Medal with the Combat "V" for combat service in my 2nd Brigade Platoon in Kuwait. The citation contained terms such as "minimizing potential hostile consequences" and "neutralizing the threat" which was just a Marine Corps speak for doing a great job and killing a bunch of Iraqi soldiers. The award did not reach my desk before we were released from active duty, so I decided to give it to him at the West Los Angeles Police Division where he was assigned. The command staff and a great many of his fellow police officers were present, and the local police booster association provided refreshments. It was a great honor for me to present the medal to a very surprised young man.

I would run across "R. J." from time to time, and was very proud of him. He ultimately went to Metropolitan Division and became a well-respected member of the SWAT team. He remained in the Marine Corps Reserve and attained the rank of sergeant major. He was mobilized several times for combat service in Iraq and Afghanistan. In 2009, while in Afghanistan, Sergeant Major R. J. Cottle was killed in action. God bless you Sergeant Major.

As an interesting note, Charlie Beck, the LAPD chief at the time of this writing, obviously also holds "RJ" in great esteem, as he wears as his duty weapon the 9mm Baretta pistol that Cottle carried on the Police Department.

Parachute Jumps – Final Tally and Long-Term Consequences

Between my two tours of duty in 3D ANGLICO I completed somewhere around sixty parachute jumps. The fixed-wing aircraft that I jumped from included: C-130 Hercules, C-141 Starliner, C-123 Boxcar, OV-10 Broncos, and C17D Skytrain. The helicopters that I jumped from included: CH53 Sea Stallion, CH46 Sky Knight, and OH-1 Huey. There may have been another aircraft or so that I just do not recall. I have never been a "feather merchant" (lightweight person), but rather have always been a stocky person. Consequently, I have always descended pretty fast even after my parachute canopy opened. For the T-10 and MC1-1B 'chutes, the advertised descent was (generally) from 16 to 20 feet per second, and for the later MC1-1C 'chutes, the descent was a wonderful (again, generally) 8 to 12 feet per second.

A good number of my landings could better be described as crash landings, where the term "crash & burn" was most appropriate. I streamed in fast and landed hard a number of times, but always managed to walk away, notwithstanding a few days of limping around. Now, as I approach the "Big 70," the physical residuals of all of these jump injuries, which seemed minor at the time because of a younger and more forgiving body, are taking a certain toll. I find myself limping around once in a while and experience pain that I swear I can almost attribute to certain hard landings! No sweat, I can handle it and if given the opportunity to roll the clock back and not have been a jumper in 3D ANGLICO, I would decline the offer. I worked hard for these aches and pains and experience them with pride (and an occasional grimace!)

ANGLICO Mess Night in Utilities – SURPRISE!

This was a major prank on me, orchestrated by my great friend and then executive officer, Lieutenant Colonel Wesley May. As my command tour was winding down, the officers very considerately planned an elaborate Mess Night in my honor. These are carefully planned and executed formal dinners, with an abundance of great food, fine wine, and good cigars – a time-honored military tradition. On the appointed evening, I appeared in my finest formal "Mess Dress" uniform, as per the tradition, and was surprised that all of my officers were in the utility uniform! They wanted to make me look stupid and have fun at my expense, and it worked! It was a wonderful evening and the opportunity to spend some quality time with the fine officers that I had been honored to command.

Change of Command – Truly a Sad Day

My two-year tour as the commanding officer came to an end in July of 1991. The commanding general of the Fourth Marine Division had selected my executive officer, Lieutenant Colonel Wesley May, to succeed me as the commanding officer of 3D ANGLICO. It would have been impossible to find a better man for the job, as Wes was and is a superb human being, a great friend, and a fine Marine. Like me, Wes was a former enlisted Marine who had received a commission during the Vietnam War. Relinquishing command was a painful process, as I had found so much personal and professional satisfaction as the commanding officer of that wonderful unit. Wes and I had a little bit of fun when I passed the pole with the unit's colors to him as part of the ceremony; as he started to pull it towards him, I gently resisted and tried to pull it back towards me, resulting in big smiles on both of our faces. The truth is that I was pretty much devastated.

As I drove home after the change of command ceremony, I actually felt somewhat lost. The previous two years had been among the busiest and most rewarding of my life, and all of a sudden I went from full steam ahead to almost a dead stop. I was pretty much uncertain about what the future held for me in the Marine Corps, but was guardedly optimistic. I knew that I had done an exemplary job as the commanding officer, and I knew that everybody else recognize that as well, including the commanding general and the staff of the division in New Orleans. Although I personally did not get into combat with my advance party, I received strong accolades for the training and leadership that I provided, and was given a share of the credit for the superb actions of my men in combat during the first Gulf War. It was also recognized that the degree of training and accomplishments that my unit experienced during the period of active duty were nothing short of extraordinary. The G-3 of the division, Colonel Merrill Saxton, a great guy and strong supporter (also the recipient of a Navy Cross from the Vietnam War), had assured me that I would be welcome to join the staff of the division in New Orleans. Nevertheless, it was a time when I felt somewhat lost. Fortunately, I didn't say lost for very long and soon did in fact join the staff of the 4th Marine Division.

Medal For Top Soto – 15 Years Late!

Master Sergeant Richard Soto is one of those wonderful men who works very hard, now after retirement, to keep the spirit of his Marine Corps service alive. Like most master sergeants, he was referred to as "Top Soto." Just about every year he hosts a reunion at his house, and it is a great and enjoyable event for all of us who had the honor of serving in 3D ANGLICO.

During one of these gatherings at his house, probably around 2009, I casually asked him about the award that I knew he had to have received at the time of his retirement, as it is common to reward somebody at the end of their career with either a Meritorious Service Medal or a Navy-Marine Corps Commendation Medal to recognize superior service. I could tell that he was hurt when he answered my question and said that he never received a medal. I believe that I demonstrated some indignation, to which he replied: "Forget it colonel, just leave it alone!"

That conversation triggered an absolute resolve on my part to make sure that he got a medal! I did not realize how long the process was going to take and just how difficult it was going to be. Since he had been retired for more than five years, Marine Corps regulations stipulate that the medal recommendation had to come through a member of Congress. After having put together a pretty comprehensive package recommending the award of a Meritorious Service Medal, I processed the package through the office of then-Representative Jane Harman. Her office passed it on to the Marine Corps Congressional Liaison Officer who then forwarded the entire package to Headquarters Marine Corps.

Between the various award boards convened both at Headquarters Marine Corps and the Secretary of the Navy, it took over two years of rewrites, soliciting additional endorsements, resubmitting to various boards, and every other imaginable delay. Finally, the Secretary of the Navy Commendations Board recommended, and Headquarters Marine Corps concurred, in awarding Master Sergeant Soto the Navy-Marine Corps Commendation Medal. Top Soto was unaware that this effort was even underway, but his wife was continually aware and worked with me on the project. When the medal was finally sent to me, I set up a surprise ceremony at 3D ANGLICO. I told Top Soto that I was going to receive a medal and that I wanted him present because of all the support that he provided to me when I was the commanding officer.

Top Soto's wife and I got a hold of as many of our old associates as possible and at the end of a drill on a Sunday afternoon in August, 2011, when we were all assembled, and Soto thought that I was about to be called up, we called up Top Soto. Retired Colonel Wesley May, Soto's wife, and I all participated in pinning the medal on his chest as the citation was being read. He was surprised and I know deeply appreciative. We all then went to Soto's house where his wife had prepared a surprise celebration and buffet dinner. It was a lot of work and a lot of effort, but something that I just had to do for a man who had served in the Marine Corps, and me personally, so well for so long.

Chapter Twenty-One
4th MARINE DIVISION STAFF (4th MARDIV)

In the late summer of 1991, after a very successful two-year tour as the commanding officer of 3D ANGLICO, I transferred to the staff of the 4th Marine Division, in New Orleans, Louisiana. At that time, I was part of a very small "battle staff" of seasoned personnel who the commanding general could dispatch to large exercises and perform the role of a division headquarters.

Transferring to the "Big Easy"

My stock was pretty good with the commanding general and staff of the Marine Reserve Forces headquarters in New Orleans. A true sponsor and dear friend was Colonel Merrill Sexton, the chief of staff and a Navy Cross recipient from the Vietnam War. For a good part of my ANGLICO tour he was the assistant chief of staff-operations, G-3 and the person to whom I reported. We had a mutual fondest and respect for one another, and he made it clear that I would be a welcome addition to the reserve division staff being assembled in New Orleans, as a reorganization was underway and a true "battle staff" made up of solid reservists, as opposed to the then existing administrative staff made up of regular personnel, would soon be assembled. Within a month or so, I was assigned and doing my weekend drills in New Orleans, and was further assigned as the Division's Operations Officer working for the G-3, a reserve colonel and employee of State Children's Services from El Paso, Texas, Jim Preston. Jim is a great fellow and to this day, a dear friend. Our families have visited and vacationed together, and Cathy and Jeanne are close as well. One of our bonds was our commitment to foster kids; Jim and Jeanne had adopted three foster kids! We worked well together on several exercises and other activities.

An interesting thing about this assignment is that I had to travel to and from New Orleans, for reserve drill weekends, at my own expense! Drill travel is something each reservist pays on his or her own, as the rules pretty much assume that reservist drill at a unit close to their homes, and the drill pay is assumed to have an adequate built-in allowance for this consideration. For high-ranking folks like myself, this was a price that we had to pay for the honor of the positions that we held. The result was that I devoted my drill pay to airline travel. However, when called to active duty for training, special meetings, conferences, or investigations – in New

Orleans (NOLA) or anywhere else – orders were issued and the government paid for travel.

Professional Military Education (PME)

Although I did not attend Officers Candidate School (OSC) or The Basic School (TBS), I attended just about everything else! During my Marine Corps career as an officer I attended several intelligence courses, just about every amphibious course offered at the Naval Amphibious School at Coronado, Air Support Control School at 29 Palms, Air Force Command & Staff in Alabama, Parachute Course in Georgia, Amphibious Warfare School in Quantico, Marine Corps Command & Staff College also in Quantico, Armed Forces Staff College in Virginia, and the Naval War College in Rhode Island. Many of these were the abbreviated reserve versions involving several in-residence sessions and correspondence. There were also lesser courses and schools too numerous to mention. Certainly, this PME contributed to my successful career.

Broken Heart Over Stolen Iwo Jima Maps

To this day, I remain livid over this issue. My dear friend Ben Staffer (RIP), who had been a sergeant in the 4th Tank Battalion during the Battle for Iwo Jima, gave me a series of maps that he carried ashore during that epic battle. I suggested and he enthusiastically agreed that the maps would be provided to the commanding general of the III Marine Expeditionary Force (III MEF) on Okinawa, which was the Marine command over that part of the world, and from where PME (professional military education) trips to Iwo Jima were often initiated. Elaborate plans were made for the maps to be displayed on the walls in the hallway outside the office of the commanding general, and they were sent to Okinawa with a major who acted as a courier.

A couple of years later, Ben asked how the maps were received by the battle staff, and when I passed on the inquiry to the III MEF chief of staff, he claimed no knowledge of the maps. Somebody made off with these historic maps and no doubt wanted to display them in his home, or worse yet to sell them. I have a suspicion as to who that person is, but have no way of knowing for sure that he is the one who took the maps. The pain of this treachery remains in my craw.

Sleazy Cabbie With Porn for the Passengers

This is not the typical chamber of commerce business practice, but not real surprising given the unique culture of the Greater New Orleans area, and the devil-may-care attitude of many of the folks who live there. One day I hailed a cab to take me from my hotel in Metairie to the airport. After learning my destination, the cab driver handed me a very large three-ring binder, then hit the gas and took off for my destination. The binder was full of pictures of naked women, pages and pages of them, in every conceivable position and representing every imaginable ethnicity. While not embarrassed or offended (I was long past those hang-ups!), this was not the reading material I would have selected, but I politely scanned the pages (with perhaps a pause or two!) before handing the binder back to him. This was obviously a technique that he used with male passengers to get a good tip; because of the ingenuity, I recall being a bit more generous with the tip than usual.

Visit to Lieutenant General Chesty Puller's Tomb

Chesty Puller is among the giants of the Marine Corps. His service stemmed from World War One, Banana Wars, pre-war China, World War Two, and Korea. He retired in 1956, and was the recipient of five Navy Crosses. Books have been written about this great Marine. During one of my many trips to the Marine Base at Quantico, Virginia, I decided to make a pilgrimage to his final resting place, in Saluda, Virginia. On top of his tomb was resting a freshly starched camouflage USMC cover (hat) and three connected shiny silver stars, denoting the rank of lieutenant general. It was clear that some Marine provided daily maintenance to Chesty Puller's tomb. It was my honor and privilege to pay that visit and show my respects for one of my heroes.

Plank Holder in the New 4th Division Staff

When I first transferred to New Orleans, I was actually assigned to the Headquarters of the Marine Reserve Forces, to serve in various capacities, but primarily to be part of a battle staff that would be assembled for exercises. After a year or so in New Orleans, Marine Forces Reserve (MARFORRES) was reorganized to actually create both a 4th Division staff and a 4th Air Wing staff. We got a general and a bunch of dedicated billets, and some solid focus. At that time I became the deputy assistant G-3, working for a colonel (I was still a lieutenant colonel), Joe Sawyer, a good fellow and attorney from Alabama. While Joe did a fine job and became a good friend, I was saddened that my good pal Jim Preston did not get the G-3 position.

In the musical chairs that occurred, a couple of years later I became the G-3 "actual" (assistant chief of staff, operations), then later the inspector general (assistant chief of staff, readiness G-7). Frankly, we were a pretty flexible group of senior officers, all with a ton of experience, including command time. When tasks or exercises arose, we would often pick the person, notwithstanding his or her present billet, who was either the most qualified or available, or both. Because there were so few of us, this flexibility was truly a necessity.

Promoted to Colonel

As someone who doubted he would ever make corporal, making full colonel was quite a humbling event. I was given a date when the ceremony was to be held, on a weekend, and took Cathy with me to New Orleans that month. After the ceremony, conducted in the office of the commanding general but not a big extravaganza, Colonel Jim and Jeanne Preston joined us for a fun lunch in the French Quarter. I still couldn't believe that I actually had eagles on my collar! I wish my parents and brother could have been present, but my mom was in a nursing home and both my father and brother had passed away many years prior.

Sitting in a Box of Kitty Litter Under a Sun Lamp

With all of my Marine Corps service, I have spent a considerable amount of time at the Marine Corps Air Ground Combat Center at Twentynine Palms, California. It is a very big place, consisting of close to 1,000 square miles of the California desert. Although there is a built-up portion of the base with many buildings, schools, bowling alley, gym, headquarters, etc., etc., 99 percent of the base is raw desert.

The base started out as an Army Air Corps glider training facility during World War II, was dormant for a while, and was given to the Marine Corps in the late 1950s. When I joined the staff of the 4th Marine Division, I started seeing a lot more of "The Stumps" as the base is sometimes called. I probably participated in a least a dozen (maybe more) two-week Combined Arms Exercises (CAX) in the 1990s. Working and practicing combat skills in 120-degree heat while wearing full combat gear, including a flak vest and helmet, is a real character builder. I could think of places I would rather have been, but few that were as well suited for training realistic to the future threats facing our nation.

Cokes for the Road Guards

I never forgot where I came from, and as an officer believed that I was always kind and considerate to the troops, with the exception of those instances when I dealt with troublesome and disciplinary issues. I don't think I every returned a salute without providing a smile and a "thank you." I did then and continue to have enormous warmth and respect for enlisted Marines. Without understanding my emotions, even as I type this paragraph, my eyes are watering up with emotion.

Something I really liked to do, and did it often and almost obsessively, was to provide young troops with surprise refreshments. Our exercises, of which I participated in many, were usually in the middle of the summer when the temperature was 120 degrees in the shade, and there wasn't any!

I often found frequent excuses (at my rank, I really did not need an excuse!) to leave the field and go main side (a good meal, PX, fart around, or whatever). When returning to the field, I would very often go first to the Oasis Café and get a dozen or so large Cokes with ice, and given them to the road guards and other young Marines manning isolated posts under the blazing sun. The appreciation was evident on the faces of the Marines when I handed the Coke out the window, but most looked a bit puzzled as well; having a full colonel emerge out of nowhere with a Coke for a junior enlisted man was not a common occurrence! God bless those wonderful young men, and I am grateful that I had the honor to lead and support them.

Air-to-Ground Encryption – It Just Did Not Happen

A very key and critical issue in the conduct of combat operations is the ability to have secure communications. This is accomplished by using special equipment to encrypt radio transmissions.

Unfortunately, during my entire time in the Marine Corps, this was easier said than done; the equipment was pretty complicated and prone to failure. I realize that there are those who would disagree with this assessment, but from my perspective in the trenches, encryption just did not work out.

As I reflect on this reality, I don't think I ever participated in an exercise where we did not plan to encrypt, but never once did it ever come to pass. In the fog of training and all the challenges that went along with complicated activities, all the effort that would have gone into encryption efforts would have measurably detracted from all of the other things we needed to accomplish. Fortunately, things have changed and encryption is not now the hassle that it used to be. Thank goodness, as this is a critical area and the last thing that combat Marines need is for the bad guys to be listening to our radio transmissions.

Foolish Behavior Necessitated Dangerous Med-Evac in High Winds

Marines are not immune to stupid and immature behavior, and sometimes people will do things so foolish as to endanger the lives of other people. I was the witness to the potential catastrophic consequences of such behavior one very dark summer evening at the top of OP Crampton at the Marine Corps Base at Twentynine Palms. It was an *extremely* windy night and we were on an outcropping several thousand feet above the desert floor. A young lance corporal decided that he would kill a rattlesnake by squirting lighter fluid on it, with the dispenser acting like a flamethrower. First of all, this was just stupid and immature, and we did not need to screw with the snakes; ignore them and generally speaking they will ignore you. Secondly, he failed to realize that he was spraying lighter fluid into the wind, and igniting it as it left the container. He ended up spraying burning lighter fluid all over himself, and sustained some very serious burns over a good portion of his body, much of it having been exposed because it was so hot (middle of the summer) that his clothing was minimal.

Realistically, the only way to get him off the OP and to medical treatment was via helicopter, but to do so in the dark with the horrific winds was very dangerous. Nevertheless, the two pilots who were on call at the main part of the base for emergency med-evacs decided to try to get him off that mountain. We were all so pissed at the kid we were damn near ready to let him die, but obviously did not take that approach. After several efforts, the Huey helicopter (UH-1) managed to touch down, load him on board, and transport him to the base hospital. I know that he did not die, but beyond that I do not know what his fate was. He was badly burned and I am sure required a considerable amount of prolonged medical care.

Commended by the Commandant Of The Marine Corps

One of the professional highlights of my Marine Corps career was being personally and warmly commended by General Mundy, the Command-ant of the Marine Corps (CMC), for my performance as the Assistant Chief of Staff (G-3) during a Combined Arms Exercise (CAX) at the MCAGCC, Twentynine Palms. I was the fellow who planned and orchestrated the activities of scores of aircraft, armored vehicles, and hundreds of men in a very successful and realistic amphibious combat exercise. Not bad for someone who once doubted that he would ever go beyond private first class!

Assigned as Inspector General – But Different Than Most

As I completed my tour as the assistant chief of staff, G-3, Brigadier General Fred Lopez, a long-time friend and now the commanding general of the 4th Marine Division, asked me if I was interested in becoming the Inspector General of the 4th Marine Division, the official title being Assistant Chief of Staff, G-7 (Readiness). I told General Lopez that I would be honored to assume that position, however I diplomatically indicated a condition that I felt was essential if I was to take on the position: that a deficient report by me or my personnel would not result in adverse action against the commanding officer of the inspected unit unless there was intentional misconduct, fraud, or clearly negligent performance, and that I would have the ability to mobilize "assist" teams to help a unit get up to acceptable performance before finalizing my inspection report. In the past, it was not unusual for the previous commanding general of Marine Forces Reserve to order the relief of a commanding officer based on deficient inspection results, and it was my opinion that some of those reliefs were unnecessary and inappropriate. General Lopez shook my hand and said that he saw things in exactly the same light. I became the inspector general.

In the approximately two years that I held this position, my section conducted scores of various types of inspections, including MORDTs (Mobilization Organizational Readiness Deployment Tests), which were unannounced and greatly feared. My biggest challenge was making sure that the personnel who constituted my inspection team manpower, most of whom were in various reserve staff groups throughout the nation, deferred to my leadership and direction. These were good people, mostly senior field-grade officers, including several full colonels, who were used to performing inspections and having the final say in the results, as opposed to now falling under the cognizance of the commanding general of the 4th Marine Division, which meant working for me. There were a few spirited discussions, but using a combination of goodwill, persuasion, education, and just a tad bit of authority, I got things under control and pretty much smoothed out among all the inspectors.

During my tenure, not one commanding officer was relieved because of inspection results. It was the norm, rather than the exception, for me to put my people in the assist mode, as opposed to the inspection mode, immediately upon arrival. Also, it was very common for me to call Headquarters and get approval for "man-days" authorization, the military equivalent of overtime, for the unit to bring some personnel in to assist in resolving a problem area discovered during the inspectional period. I was proud to say that my inspection reflected the state of the unit at the time the team departed, not at the time it arrived. Needless to say, I was well thought of throughout the division for compassion and common sense. My previous experience as an enlisted Marine absolutely contributed to my approach in these types of activities.

Painful Investigation of a Fellow Colonel

This was nasty and painful. During a two-week period at 29 Palms, in a large tent out in the middle of the desert, one of my fellow colonels, who was known as a very religious man and a non-drinker, did something that ended his promising career. He got drunk with a bunch of enlisted Marines, switched collar insignias with a sergeant, participated in singing truly raunchy songs, and hoisted a female nurse (lieutenant) in the air and paraded around the tent while holding her in his arms – against her will and despite her protests. She made a formal complaint and it was given to me to investigate.

It was what it was and despite my efforts to be as helpful as I could to his defense attorney, he was forced into retirement. Fortunately, he was allowed to retire as a full colonel, but probably six or so years before mandatory retirement. He had been the executive officer of an aviation squadron during the First Gulf War and had just been elevated to the presidency of a very significant military support organization, and there had been a very good chance – prior to this incident – that he would have been among the very few to actually promote to the rank of general.

The pain that I felt for him was somewhat minimized as I was aware and had been troubled by a "dark side" to him that some others had not seen. About a year prior, to keep from being embarrassed over a relatively minor issue, he flat-out lied to a general and said that he had made a notification to a major on an issue, when in fact I was absolutely aware that he had not made the notification. At the time, and in the presence of the general, I diplomatically corrected him; to which he responded – incorrectly – that it was me who was wrong. His actions had the potential, had I not intervened, to be damaging to the major's career. I was very troubled by this behavior, and it was especially puzzling because of the overt way that he wore his Christianity on his sleeve. I believe that he was morally corrupt, with variable ethics, and that his forced retirement was in the Corps' best interests.

Paying Dues to be in the Marine Corps Reserve?

As the inspector general, some unique situations came my way, but few were more unique than an informal and back-channel inquiry to a general from the suspicious wife of a captain in one of the Division's subordinate units. I think it came to me because no one else wanted to have to provide some very bad news to the wife of a young officer. She had become concerned about his frequent drill weekends and a questionable budgetary situation. She had been assured by her husband that he was required to attend two full reserve drill weekends per month and, instead of reserve drill pay, actually had to pay dues to be in the military reserve! It was not a pleasant discussion, but the buck stopped with me. The wife was clearly not happy, but I think she pretty much knew that her husband was an idiot. The captain was not well thought of by his commanding officer, and I suspect that both the marriage and his Marine Corps career didn't last much longer.

Troubling Information About a General (Select)

I still don't know the whole story on this situation. There was a fellow colonel on the staff, who in civilian life was married and an attorney in the Midwest. His closest associate was the colonel who was forced into retirement over the escapade involving hoisting the Navy nurse in the air while drunk. This particular colonel was among several of us who were in the zone for consideration for promotion to brigadier general. As a fairly junior colonel, I knew that I was not really competitive for this selection board; the colonel in question was competitive, along with several others.

There was very clearly a growing sense of anticipation about the potential selection of this particular colonel, and it was really puzzling to me and to others. He continually discussed the issue with passion. The later disgraced colonel, who was a key player in an influential Marine Corps reserve association, discussed the matter as if it was likely that this colonel would be selected. Finally, the commanding general and the assistant division commanding general, both fine gentlemen and great Marines, also discussed this same colonel – to the exclusion of the other colonels – with the same sense of anticipation. It was obvious that things were happening behind the scenes, and most likely that these two generals had been pushing – again behind the scenes – the selection board to select this particular colonel for promotion.

Well, it happened; the selection board results were announced and he was one of about four reserve colonels, from a total of probably four hundred reserve colonels, who was selected for promotion to brigadier general. It was no surprise. I was at a loss as to just how this all occurred, as it was inconsistent with fairness and procedures, as I understood the process to be. Now I think I have figured it out: politics at the highest levels play a major role in general officer promotions.

I had real reservations about this guy, and at one time even considered sharing some of my observations with one of the two generals who later became a real sponsor of his. He was incredibly bright and knowledgeable about the Corps and complex operational strategies and processes, but seemed to be weak in essential character traits. I felt he was reckless, immature, and that he had a sense of inappropriate entitlement based on his rank.

First, he drove like a teenager with his first automobile; frequently gunning the engine and racing around corners on two wheels; not the kind of behavior you would associate with a mature adult. Secondly, I had a very strong sense that he was engaged in extramarital affairs that had the potential to blow up in his face and be an embarrassment to the Corps; a matter that first came to my attention based on somewhat cryptic comments made by not-too-happy-with-him Navy nurses when I investigated the aforementioned disgraced colonel. Finally, as people did nice things for him, he barely acknowledged their actions; a matter that really hit me when I shipped an entire box of antique Marine Corps uniforms to him for his collection and never even got a thank you. I had the sense that he felt he could pretty much do as he pleased and that some of the rules that pertained to the rest of us did not pertain to him.

A couple of other issues, in hindsight, should probably have derailed this fellow's promotion. On at least one occasion, I believe after selection but before pinning on his star, one of the two generals became aware that this colonel was focusing inappropriate attention on a female major, and quietly told him to knock it off. Also, it was fairly common knowledge that he and, again, the later disgraced colonel engaged in some type of troubling behavior while on a deployment to Korea, but that it never became an official matter.

Subsequent to his promotion to brigadier general, he became the commanding general of a reserve command, and within about a year all of these weak character traits exploded in his face, and did in fact bring discredit to the Marine Corps. As a commanding general, he became engaged in a sexual relationship with the wife of a Marine sergeant (violating the wife of an enlisted Marine is beyond a mortal sin in the USMC!), and then when confronted with the issue lied to his boss, a lieutenant general. There were other problems with his behavior and actions as well, as his true character deficiencies came back to the surface, but they paled in comparison to his actions with the wife of an enlisted man. He was relieved of command, demoted back to colonel, and forced to retire from the Marine Corps. Then, authorities in his state charged him with state tax evasion, convicted him, and put him on criminal probation. It is unfortunate that he cast the Corps in an unpleasant light.

I continue to feel pain for the two generals who I know really went to bat to get this guy promoted to brigadier general. Both are truly wonderful men that I respect greatly, and I have every confidence that they truly believed that this person was the best, brightest, and most deserving. While the opportunity is not likely to arise, and if it did the pain would probably prevent a candid discussion on this issue, I would really like to hear the whole story on this person from one of those two generals who influenced his promotion. Knowing that they orchestrated the promotion of a person who brought such discredit to the Corps, and that in so doing prevented the promotion to general of a more deserving person, had to be very painful for these two gentlemen. Like me, both of these generals have been retired for a number of years.

I have asked myself several times if I should have shared my reservations about this person, who was a colleague and potential competitive officer, with one or both of the two generals who were clearly his sponsor. On one hand, the information would certainly have been of value. However, the information may well have been poorly received and seen as biased and coming from a disgruntled promotional competitor. Also, for a person to step outside the box and be this candid with a general about another high ranking person would have been somewhat outside the norm of acceptable interaction. It was also very clear that these two generals really liked this guy, so in all likelihood the only victim from such a candid discussion would probably have been me!

As I teach leadership and mentor high-ranking law enforcement officials, I frequently think of this situation as I consider the dilemma of how to select those people you choose to intensely mentor and push up in various organizations. This experience has influenced me in arriving at a couple of additional criteria to be applied in determining whether someone is worthy of being pushed up professionally. First, does he or she have credibility with their peers? This fellow looked good to his superiors, but not to his peers. Secondly, is he or she someone who routinely does thoughtful things for others when there is not likely to be any personal payoff? Again, this fellow would have flunked this test big time; everything was for him and about him.

Exonerating an Innocent Colonel

As the inspector general, it was my responsibility, circumstances permitting, to personally conduct sensitive investigations involving fellow colonels. A female gunnery sergeant, who was a regular Marine assigned to a regimental inspector-instructor staff within the 4th Division, filed a formal complaint of sexual harassment against the regimental commanding officer and a male gunnery sergeant. She alleged direct harassment by her gunnery sergeant colleague in the administrative section, and biased treatment because of her gender and ethnicity (she was a minority) by the regimental commanding officer. The colonel who was the focus of the allegations had just gotten orders to a coveted assignment at the Pentagon; obviously those orders were placed in abeyance pending the outcome of my investigation. I was assigned to personally conduct the investigation, and actually had to make several trips to the regimental headquarters during the inquiry.

It did not take long to realize that her accusations were totally without merit. It was she who had acted inappropriately in a variety of situations. When she started to experience the very predictable consequences of her poor performance and behavior, she in turn tried to turn herself into a victim. Unfortunately, during my police and military careers, this is not the first time I encountered this type of troublesome behavior. *Some* of the actions that triggered the consequences she found troubling included her not always showing up for work as scheduled, truly deficient performance in the conduct of critical administrative tasks, inappropriate use of a government credit card, and failing to take physical fitness tests as directed and required. However, based on the sensitive nature of sexual harassment and the potential likelihood that my investigation would be closely scrutinized, I was determined to ensure that it was the most comprehensive investigation ever seen by the Judge Advocate General (JAG) in Marine Forces Reserve (MARFORRES), which was the higher headquarters over the 4th Marine Division.

My investigation not only completely disproved her allegations, but also uncovered additional problematic actions on her part. First, the *scores* of interviews made clear that her conduct and performance was totally substandard and unacceptable for a person of her rank, and that she lacked the knowledge required of her position. Among a variety of uncomplimentary actions was my discovery that she had falsified a note from a physician to indicate that she should be excused from physical activities! My report and investigative findings were as solid as could be, and were cited by the JAG as comprehensive and irrefutable. In addition to finding her allegations without merit, I made several recommendations pertaining to her, including additional training, closer supervision, and an evaluation of her physical fitness for continued military service.

Not surprisingly, she tried to torpedo my investigation. As a prominent member of the Women Marine's Association (WMA), she went directly to a female general who had a reputation for special interest in women's issues, and whom some thought was unrealistically sympathetic to gender allegations (I do not know if this was accurate). This female general obviously went straight to my general, as a copy of my investigation (about four inches thick!) ended up on his desk, and it had numerous yellow stick'um notes scattered throughout the pages. My commanding general, who had just replaced the former general, was known as very political and someone who, in my opinion, would not have hesitated to sacrifice me if he could advance his standing with this particular female general.

Somewhat boldly, but diplomatically, I entered his office and, while pointing to my investigation, feigned surprise that he had a copy (it had previously been approved by the outgoing commanding general and forwarded to the JAG) and asked if he had any questions. He said he had no questions, and that was *almost* the end of the issue. This new commanding general brought in with him a new chief of staff, a colonel who was the same ethnicity as the female gunnery sergeant. During transitional discussions, this colonel commented that any investigation as thick as the one that I had conducted most assuredly had to be a "cover up" of some sort. I cannot think of a time when I came closer to knocking a fellow Marine officer on his ass!

The "hold" on the proposed reassignment of the regimental commanding officer was lifted and he did receive his new coveted assignment at the Pentagon. I never did follow up to determine the fate of the female gunnery sergeant, but am quite certain that her allegations, which I proved to be without merit, and the new issues about her that stemmed from my findings, did not do her career any good.

Disappointed With The New Commanding General

I chose to leave the 4th Division staff when a newly promoted general, who I thought poorly of, became the commanding general. This fellow, in my judgment, reflected the epitome of troubling general officer politics. When this man was initially promoted, there was widespread disappointment and outrage as it was painfully clear that his promotion was based on politics, favoritism, and beltway intrigue as opposed to performance and merit. Just about his entire career as a senior officer was spent in a staff group assignment, and not out in the commands and trenches like the rest of us. He had been a senior aide to a United States senator and had superb contacts at the highest levels of government. I am certain that he took and/or orchestrated actions that benefitted the Marine Corps, but like just about everyone else I felt that promotion to general officer, over much more qualified and deserving colonels, should not have been his reward. It was well known that he had a superb relationship with the commandant and other senior general officers. These superb contacts were obvious during his tenure as a general officer, and continued right up to his retirement extravaganza, and fueled cynicism of the general officer promotion process. I remain surprised that the top leadership of the Corps was not more sensitive to the impression this troubling issue created in the minds of many.

I was displeased when he was assigned as my commanding general. At the time, I was the inspector general and one of his several key staff officers. Without any conflict or rancor, I was not impressed with his demeanor during the single weekend drill that we served together, and I decided that I did not want to serve as one of his top people. I contacted the commanding general of the I MEF Augmentation Command Element (MACE) at Camp Pendleton, who had previously offered me an assignment, and arranged for transfer to that command.

I must confess that my impression of this person was likely tainted by my disdain for the process that caused him to be promoted. While far from the most worthy and deserving, I am sure that he was basically a good person and an honorable Marine.

Investigating a Tragedy on the Mexican Border

A terrible tragedy occurred along the Rio Grande River in the community of Redford, Texas. Four Marines who were loaned to JTF-6 (Joint Task Force) out of El Paso, who were deployed in a alleged concealed "hide site" to watch for narcotic smugglers, shot and killed an 18-year-old man who was herding his goats. The subsequent investigations, very controversial because of the involvement of ethnic and immigrants rights groups, revealed the matter to be an unfortunate unintentional tragedy.

The young man saw the Marines, who were dressed in bizarre camouflage outfits, out in the area where he herded his goats, and he fired a couple of .22 rounds in their direction; in self defense, one of the Marines fired back and killed the lad. Headquarters contacted me, at the time the marshal of San Bernardino County, to go on active duty and lead the investigation, which I was certainly capable of doing. However, it was then decided to add a Marine lawyer (JAG), who had an assistant who was also a lawyer to the team.

Before it was over, a two-star general who was also a lawyer (and a great guy notwithstanding some disagreements), was put in charge of the team. In my judgment, the effort became bureaucratic cluster fornication! Politics took precedence over the practical, and form became more important than substance. The key attorney (nice guy), who was a lieutenant colonel, spent literally hours each day on the phone talking with attorneys at Headquarters Marine Corps, with every step we took being discussed and vetted by a distant group of attorneys.

The final straw for me occurred on the ground at the shooting site when we most likely found the shell casings from the rifle the kid used to fire on the Marines; when the Presidio County Sheriff's Department declined to get involved and book the shell casings as evidence, the combined legal troika decided that they should remain where they were on the ground; my pleas to photograph them in place, then carefully gather and send them to the Texas Department of Public Safety fell on deaf ears.

Before it was over, the lieutenant colonel insisted on rewriting even my interview notes for consistency with his writing style. I found a way of disengaging from this investigation a bit prematurely. This experience was among several that convinced me of the inappropriateness of having a lawyer lead an investigation. They were all good people with good intentions, but the process should have been lead by an experienced and talent investigator, with significant legal support. This matter was largely resolved through tighter rules governing military participation with federal law enforcement authorities, strengthened training, and a monetary settlement to the family of the victim.

Chapter Twenty-Two
I MARINE EXPEDITIONARY FORCE – AUGMENTATION COMMAND ELEMENT
(I MEF ACE)

In mid-1997, after approximately six years on the staff of the 4th Marine Division, I transferred to the Augmentation Command Element of the 1st Marine Expeditionary Force at Camp Pendleton, as the head of the Operations Group. This outfit was essentially a recruiting and training entity for senior officers and senior enlisted personnel, with the mission of preparing senior personnel for key positions to augment deployment with the I MEF. In additional to potential activation at some point, there were always exercises and other events where some degree of augmentation was necessary, and the folks in this outfit got quite a lot of experience with their active duty counterparts.

My Last Marine Corps Assignment

My last assignment in the Marine Corps was Head, Operations Group, I MACE at Camp Del Mar. I enjoyed this assignment, and felt that I made a real and positive difference in attracting and preparing some outstanding folks for augmentation when it was needed. It was close to home, at the beach, and I had the opportunity to work with some fine people. My last commanding general was Brigadier General Frank Quinlan, a friend and great guy who treated me very well.

I actually put in my retirement papers in July of 1998, which was several months before the date that I had to retire. I did this for unselfish reasons. We were starting to ramp up for a critical exercise in Korea, and my mandatory retirement date in mid-1999 pretty much coincided with the end of that exercise. It seemed a waste to invest all that training and preparation expertise in a person who was on the very brink of retirement. Also, it was hard to get up my typical enthusiastic head of steam over this particular deployment, as I knew the effort would be wasted and it would be my swan song. As a result, I applied for retirement effective the same month that the extensive planning process was due to commence. There was another reason as well; I wanted to go out "on top" when all was well. I was still badly stinging from the poor manner in which I was treated when retiring from another organization that I loved, the Los Angeles Police Department, and felt it was the right time to go, when all was well and positive.

Retirement From The Marine Corps

It was my desire to have a low-key retirement, but one that involved all ranks, from private to general, in a somewhat casual setting where I would be given the opportunity to share my thoughts with all of my fellow Marines. Given my rank and service, I was entitled to a very formal ceremony with a parade where the entire unit would "pass in review" in honor of the retiree. While I may have been a colonel, I still recalled what a pain it was for all the troops to have to rehearse and be involved in parade practice in preparation for such an event. Had I exercised this option, the drill weekend would have been dominated with practice and preparation for my retirement ceremony. I wanted no part of such formality.

Instead, I asked only to be given the opportunity, in a "school circle" setting (informally gathered around me in a shady area), to address *all* the Marines. I wanted my family present as well. I specifically requested that the uniform of the day (again my call) be the utility uniform (the most casual). Finally, I asked that everyone of every rank be my guest at the officer's club, after my remarks, for beverages and heavy hors d'oeuvres. General Quinlan honored my desires, and it was a great experience. I spoke to all the troops about the Corps, the honor of serving, the need for every person to be proficient in their occupational fields, and I strongly encouraged all to remain in the reserves. Cathy and my adult children were present. After my remarks, we all retired to the Officer's Club for a most enjoyable and casual event. Cathy and I then drove home where, for the last time, I took off my Marine uniform.

Chapter Twenty-Three
POST USMC RETIREMENT
THOUGHTS & ACTIONS

Prior to the early 1970s, just about every physically fit young man served in the military. Except for different types of deferments (married with kids, full-time college student, or juice with someone on the local draft board), young men either enlisted in the branch of their choice or were drafted for two years into the Army. While I am extremely pro-military, I also recognize that the military, while a very good thing, is not the only way to serve your country or to gain exceptional skills, and I am not the least bit critical of those who did not serve, except for intentional draft dodgers when the draft was in effect.

The military has yielded some of the very finest men that I have ever had the honor of associating with; however, it has also yielded some of the biggest jerks I have ever known. Bottom line is that I think the military is of tremendous value in the acquisition of unique skills and perspectives, but clearly realize that these same qualities can also be acquired in other ways. With respect to women who have served; ladies, you are truly extraordinary and, generally speaking, acquired superb skills and perspectives that your sisters will never know.

Truly Wonderful Pals from the "Greatest Generation"

This entry is written with a combination of gratefulness and sadness; grateful for the friendships, but sad that just about all of my World War II USMC pals have made that transition to eternal life. My LAPD pal, Ben Staffer, was at Saipan, Roi Namur, and hit Iwo Jima on the 3rd Wave. My Glendora pal Jack Claven got hit at Iwo. My Eagle Rock pal Ed Mitchell and other LAPD pal Fred Cook were both with the 2nd Marine Division and – as I recall – hit the beaches at Tarawa and Okinawa. These folks were like big brothers to me, and men that I truly loved, respected, and very much enjoyed having as friends and mentors. God bless you Marines. Heaven is a better place because you are there guarding the streets, and I am a better man because I had the honor to have each of you in my life.

Return To The Corps and Orders to Iraq

Subsequent to the events of September 11, 2001 - where four planes were hijacked by Muslim extremists, with two flown into the World Trade Center, a third into the Pentagon, and a fourth, apparently targeted for the White House or U. S. Capitol forced down into a Pennsylvania field after a group of heroic Americans fought back against the terrorists who seized that last plane - the world changed forever. Many reservists were called up for a variety of duties, and the Marines invaded Iraq. To say that I was itching to get into the fight was an understatement; I wanted very badly to return to the Corps and do my part. However, there was a timing issue because I needed first to complete the retirement process from the San Bernardino County Sheriff's Department, where I was in my parallel law enforcement career by this time in my Marine Corps career. It was all but certain that the county intended to grant me a disability retirement because of a right hand that never completely recovered from carpel tunnel surgery.

To return to active duty and head for combat before that county process had run its course, would certainly invalidate my disability claim, even though the Marine Corps indicated that the limitations on one hand would not disqualify me for active duty. I was in the "pipeline" to rotate into Camp Fallujah as the commanding officer of an intelligence center, and had been approved/selected by then Major General Amos of the 2nd Marine Division (named as Commandant of the Marine Corps in 2010). My retirement was approved in May of 2005, and I was slated to report to Camp Pendleton no later than July 1. I had my orders in hand, had purchased new uniforms, was receiving daily briefings from the headquarters in Iraq that I was going to be part of, and had coordinated my report date with the Mobilization Unit (commanded by my good friend, Colonel Harry Williams).

About two weeks before reporting, I got an e-mail from Iraq that Headquarters, U. S. Marine Corps, had denied my request for active duty. The Marine Corps, just before I was due to report, rescinded the waiver policy for any retiree who had reached the age of 60, which was my age at the time. I was devastated then and remain broken-hearted at the inability to serve one last time.

I remain grateful that Cathy, although reluctantly, had finally agreed to support my return to the Marine Corps. The burden of our foster kids would have been hers alone, and she took it like a trooper. One benefit for her would have been a few months of not having to listen to me snore at night! I worked very hard to get myself back into acceptable physical shape, including the use of a personal trainer at a gym. I also spent a great deal of time getting myself back up to par in professional military education. Although age had taken its toll, I was back within the umbrella of acceptable physical and professional skills at the time the waiver rule was rescinded. I am still pissed about this!

Employer Support for the Guard and Reserve (ESGR)

I am honored to be able to continue to serve the defense establishment as a military representative and ombudsman for the Defense Department's Employer Support for the Guard and Reserve (ESGR). In this volunteer capacity, I occasionally brief military reserve and National Guard personnel on their rights and responsibilities as they relate to all aspects of civilian employment, and the fact that they must not suffer any form of adverse employment actions by virtue of their reserve or active military service.

I am also a trained and certified ombudsman, and often represent the Department of Defense in attempting to resolve complaints made by service personnel regarding terminations, lost promotions and/or wages, troublesome reassignments and other issues of alleged discrimination based upon military service. While some allegations are without merit, my track record in resolving legitimate allegations is just about perfect. I have found that just about all employers are pro-military and supportive of their employees who serve in the reserve or National Guard, and that most legitimate complaints are based on misunderstandings rather than malice.

There is Truly Something Special About Being a Marine!

Absolutely without denigrating other branches of the military, because they are all great, there truly is something special about being a Marine! Just about without exception, when strangers recognize each other as having been in the Marine Corps, there is an instantaneous acknowledgment and exchange of USMC-related comments, such as "what outfit were you in," etc. Instead of "goodbye," it is always, "Semper Fi!" The USMC is the great equalizer and whether it might be a couple of businessmen, a millionaire and a homeless person, or a crook and a cop, some type of bond always exists and is acknowledged when a couple of Marines come into contact with one another. I am proud to experience this reality on a daily basis.

EPILOGUE

While long retired, the Marine Corps continues to be a major force in my life. I continue to serve as a vice president with Devil Pups, am active in the Marine Corps League, and financially support the Marine Corps Reserve Association, the Marine Corps Historical Foundation, the Marine Corps Staff & Command Foundation, the Marine Corps Association, the First Marine Division Association, and just about every other Marine-oriented cause that comes my way. I am fiercely proud of my USMC service and seize just about every opportunity to demonstrate that pride to others with whom I interact. God bless the United States Marine Corps and all of those wonderful men and women, past, present, and future, who wear, or will wear, the coveted Eagle, Globe, and Anchor.

Made in the USA
San Bernardino, CA
21 September 2014